Kuṇḍalinī

Kuṇḍalinī

The SUNY Series in the Shaiva Traditions of Kashmir
Harvey P. Alper, Editor

Kuṇḍalinī

The Energy of the Depths

A Comprehensive Study Based on the Scriptures
of Nondualistic Kaśmir Śaivism

LILIAN SILBURN
Honorary Research Director
Centre National de la Recherche Scientifique

Translated by
Jacques Gontier

STATE UNIVERSITY OF NEW YORK PRESS

Published by
State University of New York Press, Albany

Printed in the United States of America

For information, address State University of New York Press,
State University Plaza, Albany, NY, 12246

Library of Congress Cataloging-in-Publication Data

Silburn, Lilian.
Kuṇḍalinī: the energy of the depths.

Translation of: La Kuṇḍalinī ou l'Energie des Profondeurs. Ed. Les Deux Océans, Paris, 1983.
Bibliography: p.
Includes index.
1. Kuṇḍalinī. 2. Kashmir Saivism—Doctrines.
I. Title. II. Title: Energy of the depths.
BL1238.56.K86S5513 1988 294.5'43 87-26762
ISBN 0-88706-800-6
ISBN 0-88706-801-4 (pbk.)

To the Serpent of the Depths
AHIRBUDHNYA

CONTENTS

Chapter 3

Chapter 4

Chapter 5

Chapter 6

Chapter 7

PART TWO
PIERCING OF THE CENTERS AND STAGES OF THE ASCENT

Chapter 1

PART THREE
THE DEEPER MEANING OF THE ESOTERIC PRACTICE

Chapter 1

Chapter 5

Kulayāga, Esoteric Sacrifice

FOREWORD

Kuṇḍalinī, the upright axis at the innermost center of a person and of the universe, is the very source of man's might, drawing and unfolding all his energies. However, rather than dwelling on the extraordinary powers acquired through her medium, the followers of the Trika, Krama, and Kaula systems lay stress on the peace and the living harmony she bestows.

Still, this mysterious energy aroused by Kuṇḍalinī yoga manifests with a violence beyond belief and cannot be manipulated without incurring certain risks.[1] Therefore, to probe into her secrets, one must seek the help of a master belonging to a special lineage and endowed with unfailing knowledge.

It cannot be overemphasized that without such a guide, or by following a powerless and ignorant teacher, the arousal of Kuṇḍalinī will have disastrous results. Very often, the serious troubles observed in some Christian mystics attributed to hysteria have no other cause than a defective ascent of Kuṇḍalinī. Should her course be diverted, such ailments as paralysis might vanish as suddenly as they had appeared, but these could well be replaced by others, such as blindness. When this is the case, one can better understand why the Śaiva masters have been so careful in this matter and have kept all these practices shrouded in mystery.

Thus there are no treatises that would offer a systematic and clear account of the practices known as esoteric (*rahasya*)—just

1. Some deviations of Kuṇḍalinī are even termed "demoniac," as they lead to depression and insanity (cf. here p. 95).

hints and glimpses scattered in different works, like haystacks in a field. All has been said, and yet only an initiated master having a comprehensive view is able to penetrate the mystery and work accordingly upon the Kuṇḍalinī energy of a true and devoted disciple. In this way, the tradition is kept alive, while its access is denied to the layman.

I did not conform myself to this custom since I have collected many of the works or sections from them dealing with Kuṇḍalinī and tried to bring out their deeper meaning. Nevertheless, I have left enough points unclarified so as not to incur the wrath of the ancient masters.

But the cryptic nature of our subject is not only the result of a deliberate will of secrecy. It is not possible to understand this yoga, which covers the whole range of mystical experiences, if one is not acquainted with the general Trika metaphysics dealing with the breaths, the word and its phonemes, the syllable *OṂ*, the mantra *SAUḤ* and various practices connected with it.

This obscurity, in fact, is derived from the very nature of the Kuṇḍalinī energy. Although she may be experienced with great intensity and bring about remarkable effects, Kuṇḍalinī cannot be grasped nor described by the intellect. Whole volumes on the subject fail to convey the slightest idea of what she really is; and yet, to those who experience her, she is as simple as Life. Better still, she is the very source of all life. But how to define life?

Although this publication brings together the Śaiva texts about Kuṇḍalinī, by no means does it disclose all her secrets; she remains as mysterious as ever. It may not be out of place to state clearly, in view of the recent growing interest aroused by the Kuṇḍalinī process, that no writings, no recipes can grant the verticality that is the sign and the fruit of an intense inner life, through which the released and fully-controlled energy becomes universalized.

Many of the ever-increasing accounts and studies on this topic do not relate to the reality of experience; they describe phenomena which, in most cases, are the products of psychic troubles, mental fantasies or of an overstrain resulting from long periods of concentration. There is a widespread but false belief that Kuṇḍalinī can be awakened through concentration on the space between the eyebrows, on the tip of the nose or on the crown of the head.

It is true that, in a few exceptional cases, a spontaneous inner experience or a sustained practice may produce some manifestations or symptoms somewhat similar to the desired experience; but at best they are only preliminary signs related to the "lower" Kuṇḍalinī: the breath goes from the back of the throat down to the center located at the base of the spine. In fact, the true Kuṇḍalinī is an upward flow of energy passing through the centers—therefore she is called "raised" Kuṇḍalinī. This ascent is a most uncommon achievement, even for the yogins who devote their life to it.

To lead Kuṇḍalinī upward successfully is not an easy task: one should not engage in such a practice without the guidance of an enlightened master and without having had access to a state of absorption. For, while a profound mystical life does not require for its development the knowledge or the practice of the ascent of Kuṇḍalinī, this practice cannot reach its complete fulfilment without a genuine mystical life. The spontaneous awakening and rising of Kuṇḍalinī becomes possible by maintaining an underlying state of recollection which has nothing to do with concentration: one should not concentrate mentally but be naturally "centered" in the heart. Trying to make Kuṇḍalinī ascend with the help of thought would be a paradox indeed, for it happens that this awakening occurs when mental activity has vanished. When the yogin has withdrawn into the state of *dhyāna*, Kuṇḍalinī can rise up to the throat; but if he wants to take her into the head, he must have the ability to remain in a deep and continuous state of absorption.[2]

For the present work, I have collected excerpts about Kuṇḍalinī which are in line with the teachings of the Kaula, Trika and Krama nondualistic schools in order to offer a coherent survey. This study consists of translations and explanatory commentaries; it draws mainly from the fundamental work of Abhinavagupta, the *Tantrāloka*, "Light on the Tantra", and from Jayaratha's gloss on the same. This is a selection which deals with the highest inner initiations of a mystical nature. Other *āgama* have also been mentioned, such as the *Vijñānabhairava*, the *Parātriṃśikā*, the *Mālinīvijaya*, all of them dear to the Kaśmirians, and dating back probably to the fourth to sixth centuries, as well as the commentaries of Kṣemarāja, a disciple of Abhinavagupta who lived at the beginning of the eleventh century, and even verses from the poetess Lallā, composed about the fourteenth century.

2. *Samādhi* or *samāveśa*.

It should be noted that this selection differs from the descriptions of *Haṭhayoga* as well as from those numerous Śaiva, Buddhist or Vaiṣṇava *tantra* that are more widely published and better known.

Part one is devoted to the nature and the various manifestations of Kuṇḍalinī, her physiology, the conditions for her awakening, rising and unfolding as experienced by the yogin, up to her ultimate cosmic expansion. This part includes excerpts translated from chapters 4 and 5 of the *Tantrāloka*.

Excerpts from a few pages of the *Tantrāloka* appear at the beginning of the second part, describing initiations known as *vedhadīkṣā*, through which the Guru, with the help of his own Kuṇḍalinī, enters the disciple's body in order to pierce its centers and allow him to experience some of the effects of the ascent of Kuṇḍalinī. A translation and an analysis of two additional texts follow:

The *Śāktavijñāna*, which is a short treatise attributed to one Somānanda, not to be confused in our opinion with the great Somānanda, master of Utpaladeva and author of the *Śivadṛṣṭi*. This work, exclusively devoted to the different stages of Kuṇḍalinī's ascent, provides a wealth of details nowhere else to be found.

The *Amaraughaśāsana* of Gorakṣanātha, though only marginally related to the Kaula and Trika schools, stands midway between those ancient schools and *Haṭhayoga*.

Part three, giving the translation of the essentials of chapter XXIX of the *Tantrāloka*, elucidates the true meaning of the esoteric path and its primordial sacrifice (*ādiyāga*), the *kulayāga*, wherein *caryākrama* is a practice associated with the rising of Kuṇḍalinī.

I wish I could have dedicated this book to Swāmi Lakshman Brahmacārin, from whom I received constant support while I was exploring the texts, but since I did not get much encouragement on his part for the publication of this work—to him a rather daring undertaking—I dedicate it to the abyssal serpent, that for thousands of years has been impatiently waiting for a sign of recognition.

INTRODUCTION

KUṆḌALINĪ YOGA
Rhythm and Vibration

The awakening of Kuṇḍalinī is, somehow, the awakening of the latent cosmic energy lying in every human being, for such an energy is the origin of all his powers, all his strength, all the forms of life he may assume.

The yoga related to Kuṇḍalinī is not a casual practice; it is responsible for the awakening, the control and the unfolding of this fundamental energy. And as such, it is part of a complete system of energy whose whole range of manifestations is, in a concrete and living manner, covered by Kuṇḍalinī under various names.

As a conscious energy, Kuṇḍalinī is at the source of the two currents that govern life: *prāṇa*, vital energy, and *vīrya*, virile potency, in the broad sense of the word. The former term denotes essentially the expanding aspect of energy, the latter its adamantine intensity. They are the two manifestations of the inmost vitality (*ojas*), from which they emerge until they blend into one energy of unique flavor (*sāmarasya*)—the bliss born from the merging of instinctual life with the inner mystical life. Thus *vīrya*, effective power, includes all forms of efficience and inspires every kind of fervor, whether of lovers, of artists or of the mystic.

This Kuṇḍalinī yoga, therefore, is the ultimate achievement on the path of energy, a higher path, complete in itself, advocated by the Kula system; but since it involves the body, it is also related to the lower path, known as the individual path.[1]

Since tantric practices aim at awakening and controlling Kuṇḍalinī, it is not possible to grasp the true meaning of Tantrism without a real knowledge of Kuṇḍalinī.

1. In his *Tantrāloka*, Abhinavagupta describes three main paths. He devotes Chapter 3 to the path of Śiva, a divine path dealing essentially with the effectiveness of the supreme mantra, the I, *AHAM*, born from the merging of the phonemes *A* (Śiva), *H* (energy), and *M* (individual). Kuṇḍalinī is viewed here as the universal, plenary energy (*pūrṇākuṇḍalinī*), not yet distinct from Śiva. Chapter 4 deals with energy (*śakti*), that of discrimination and mystical intuition, with the ascending Kuṇḍalinī (*ūrdhvakuṇḍalinī*), along with the natural causes (love, fervor) likely to promote this ascent (cf. here Part three ch. 2-3). Chapter 5 expounds the path of the individual where the means is activity; it describes in minute detail the various aspects of a yogin's experience related to the breath energy (*prāṇakuṇḍalinī*), here Part I, ch. 2 to 6.

The Dance of Śiva

"When Thou beginnest to stir, Thou unfoldest the entire universe" exclaims Utpaladeva, in praise of the dance of Śiva.
(Śivastotrāvalī XIII.15)

Śiva, the sole essence of all that exists, is also the Lord of dance (*naṭarāja*). With one of his many hands, he holds the drum, the sound vibrations of which give rise to the universe as they generate time and space; with another hand, he brandishes the fire of resorption.[1] The movement of the dance conceals his essence, as it whirls about him the flames of the manifestation, while the fire of resorption, sweeping away everything, reveals it. Standing still at the center of this twofold activity, as the seat of all power, he unfolds, with impassibility, the fiercest energies, the most antagonistic movements: emanation and resorption, concealment and grace, retraction and expansion.

His energy, the great Kālī, with whom he forms an indivisible whole, propagates to the entire universe the rhythm of this cosmic dance. Such is the essence of the Kuṇḍalinī energy, the source of all rhythms in life; what it generates is nothing but rhythm, and no level escapes it. It is in the perspective of this divine pulsation—of

1. This fire consumes the I, for this free and spontaneous mystical dance takes place in the human heart, which it fills with bliss. Many Indian sculptures show Naṭarāja dancing on a lotus pedestal, while the demon of forgetfulness, lying prostrate at his feet, gazes at him. Surrounded by a circle of flames—a symbol of his all-pervading glory—the Lord of dancers, spinning around, carries along in his whirl the entire universe. The immobility of the vertical axis around which the movement is performed stands in contrast to the intensity of the gestures of the divine dancer. May we not recognize the controlled Kuṇḍalinī in the stiff and horizontal Serpent King that, in some sculptures, Śiva is holding above his head?

which it is a privileged expression and which it reproduces at every stage—that this energy should be considered, in order to understand the role it plays within humans and in the universe.

Abhinavagupta states: "Śiva, conscious, free, and of transparent essence, is always vibrating, and this supreme energy reaches to the tip of the sense organs;[2] then he is nothing but bliss and like him the entire universe vibrates. In truth, I do not see where transmigration, a mere echo, could find a place."[3]

So the Kuṇḍalinī energy is nothing but vibration—the vibrant undulation of emanation, the more and more subtle vibration of resorption—a high-frequency vibration.

Nowadays physicists are bringing to light the importance of vibration and its fundamental role as the unifying principle; our purpose is not, however, to explain the texts in the light of modern physics. Before the ninth century of the present era, the traditions in Kashmir make mention of the vibration; they know about its power, its various forms, and seek to make its existence recognized through accurate and concrete descriptions. They speak of tremor (*calattā*), of the quivering of a fist when suddenly opened, of the first undulation on the surface of still water, of a tingle (*pipīlika*). There is such a wealth of terms referring to vibration that all their subtle shades of meaning cannot be translated.

From the root "*spand-*," to vibrate, stem the substantives *spanda, spandana*, which are generic terms, *parispanda*, intense and full subtle vibration, and also *niḥspanda*, referring to the sum total of vibrations within a given object, while *sphurattā* refers to luminous vibrations, the flashing forth of consciousness, and *nāda, dhvani*, to the vibrant resonances.

All these forms of vibrations on different frequencies are the manifestations of the Kuṇḍalinī energy in its cosmic and individual form as well. For when it is awakened, it manifests in the body in the aspect of powerful vibrations.

In a general sense, vibration corresponds to ardor and enthusiasm in all the manifestations of life: one speaks of a vibrant heart "*sahṛdaya*," whereas a lack of vibration leads to inertia as well as doubt, which depletes the energy and makes one both inefficient and dissipated.

2. Here cf. p. 152, 184 the tapered end of the sacrificial ladle out of which flows the oblation to the fire, a nectar produced by the divinized organs.

3. Quoted in M.M. śl 8 Sk, p. 196 transl. p. 90.

Rhythm

The dance of Śiva[4] suggests the primordial rhythm of the divine Heart whose pulsation initiates each and every motion in the universe.

The *Parātriṃśikā* defines the heart as the Essence of the Self, of Bhairava, and of the supreme Goddess, who is identical with him. In the center of the Heart is an etheric void, free from duality, called *vyoman* or *kha*. It is identical to the initial vibration, *spanda*. According to Abhinavagupta, this eternal, peerless heart is the still and vibrant center of Consciousness, a universal receptacle wherein all the universes are born and withdrawn. He states further: "From *kha* surges forth the nondual state of bliss where one attains the vibration (*spanda*), and to attain the *spanda* is to attain efficience." The Heart of Bhairava being undifferentiated awareness and all-pervasive, subtle vibration (*parispanda*) at the source of the ceaseless contraction and expansion of the three principal divine energies—a realm of peacefulness and supreme bliss–, heart, vibration, soaring, fervor and wave are all synonymous, for the vibration dwells in Consciousness like a wave in the ocean, and without the wave of awareness there would be nothing but a crystal-like immobility, and not an ocean of Consciousness.

Similarly, the still and ever-pure mystical heart, whose pulsation energizes all that is living, is also the resting place of Light and of still-undifferentiated Self-awareness.

Stirring and Churning of the Energy (*ksọbha* and *manthana*)

The creative emission (*visarga*) takes place when the Goddess energy, overflowing with supreme bliss, is churned by Bhairava. This churning appears as the gross aspect of vibration, as soon as Śiva differentiates himself from his energy in order to contemplate her. This is a twofold movement: a separation of Śiva and *śakti* at the time of emission, and a return into unity at the time of withdrawal.

4. The dance of Śiva illustrates the fundamental conception of Śaivism, Śiva being conscious light (*prakāśa*) and self-awareness (*vimarśa*) as the vibration of the divine Energy, Cf. M.M., Intro. p. 23-31.

As this churning produces an effervescence or an agitation of the energy, the universe gradually emerges. The one Consciousness spreads in a rhythm similar to waves unfolding one from another.

Since all the aspects of the real are in fact nothing but rhythms of the divine energy and its all-pervading vibration, the Trika and Kaula systems do not oppose matter and spirit, body and soul, microcosm and macrocosm, but recognize one original rhythm propagating freely from level to level.

In his *Pratyabhijñāhṛdaya* (*sūtra* 12-13), Kṣemarāja draws a grand epic picture of waves upon waves of energies cascading through dynamic spaces according to a fivefold process. Starting from the spatial infinity (1), they pass through the space of the heart—the center of irradiation (2), and then through the subtle space of the luminous firmament (3), through the various spatial directions (4) reaching finally the earth space (5). It is described as follows:

Citi, the divine energy, called *vāmeśvarī* because she 'emits' the universe, . . . reveals herself to the very edge of the emanation in the form of the bound subject (*paśu*). When starting to veil the Self, her highest Reality, the *cidgaganacarī* energy 'who was moving in the infinite space of Consciousness' takes the form of the slightly-limited knower; therefore she is named *khecarī*, 'who moves in *kha*,' the void within the heart. Then, concealing her essence of undifferentiated certitude, she appears as *gocarī*, 'who moves in the rays [of cognition]': the inner organ, intelligence, etc. which, as a result of a certitude of differentiation, identify the Self with differentiated objects.

When she further conceals her real nature, this energy, who consisted of the ascertainment of nondifference, becomes *dikcarī*, 'who moves in the spatial directions,' the exteriorized sense organs fit to perceive the differentiated. Finally, completely clouding her undifferentiated nature and appearing as *bhūcarī*, 'the one moving upon the earth,' she takes the form of the differentiated objective existence.

In this way, concealing her essence of universal Self, she deludes the heart of the *paśu*, the subject bound by his own energies; however, by turning inward, these same energies expand his heart and gradually reduce the alternatives—the source of duality—while unveiling the noble realm of undifferentiation (*avikalpa*), which gives access to the wonderful *bhairavīmudrā*.[5]

5. Cf. here p. 210 and seq.

Then, devouring the totality of the differentiation, the one moving in *kha* appears as a conscious and all-powerful universal agent; the one moving in the sun-rays becomes established in nondifference, the one moving in the spatial directions is immediate contemplation of nondifference, and finally the one moving upon the earth manifests the objective universe as a nectar spreading out undifferentiatedly as her own limbs (*svāṅga*). Even with a body and breaths, one reaches the state of Lord (*pati*), the agent of the fivefold activity: emanation, maintenance and withdrawal of the universe, concealment, and grace.

Return to the Heart

Thus the yogin who, through the stirring of the energy, dwells steadfastly at the junction of the twofold movement of emanation and resorption, is returned to the primordial oneness, the vibration of the universal heart.

In churning the energy[6] on every level, starting from the lowest one, Śiva takes back the divided energy, turning it inward by a series of withdrawals to the initial vibration of the peaceful Center. When all the rhythms have merged into the great rhythm of Consciousness united with Energy, the identity of Śiva and Energy is realized.

The awakening and the ascension of the most vibrant Kuṇḍalinī is therefore a gradual process of reintegration of the various levels, withdrawing into one another somewhat like rods sliding one within another or Russian dolls, one fitting into the other.[7] At every stage of the withdrawal, everything is reduced to a

6. Cf. churning of energy by Śiva or of Kuṇḍalinī by the *bindu*, here p. 11.

7. *Sampuṭīkaraṇa*. As to the encasing or the coincidence of the rhythms pertaining to the vibration or the resonance of the energies, there is no better example than the mantra *AHAṂ*. Within it the fifty phonemes of the emanation and the corresponding twenty-five levels of reality—from the first stage (*A*) to the last one (*HA*), namely Śiva and the manifested energy—finally join at one single point, the *bindu*, to produce *AHAṂ*, the universal I. There are other mantra laying the emphasis on the withdrawal, such as the sound energies of *OṂ* (cf. here p. 49) or the reascending from *bindu to bindu* (here p. 32), or else the cosmic Kuṇḍalinī (p. 81). Some aspects of this coincidence are related to the rhythms of emanation and withdrawal, cf. here p. 21, cf. also the five energies spreading by stages from *vāmeśvarī* to *bhūcarī*, here p. 8. Finally the twelve energies called *kālī* fit one into the other in twelve successive stages, the highest one containing all the others in non-difference. Cf. *Hymnes aux Kālī*, p. 80-82.

point (*bindu*), from which radiate ever greater realities as Kuṇḍalinī rises from center to center through the median channel (*suṣumnā*). The *Parātriṃśikā* sings of it in a beautiful passage (pp. 270-71): "The Heart within which everything shines gloriously and which is shining everywhere, is the one flashing light, the supreme Heart. . . . O awakened ones, adore this Heart—the universal emission—vibrating within the heart of the *suśumnā* in the great bliss of union". The union of Śiva and Śakti, of Rudra and the yoginī [on the human plane], this is "*yāmala*," the source of all our power.

Attuning all the discordant rhythms of the bound subject, Kuṇḍalinī finds anew the primordial rhythm of the *spanda* and thus attains the whole, still-undifferentiated power that confers to each of those rhythms its respective efficience, for efficience, whatever its specification, is no other than *vīrya*, a balance between two opposite movements.

Hence, the practice of Kuṇḍalinī consists in discovering the junction point between two extremes and in becoming firmly established there, at the very heart of the pulsation, a swift and subtle move from one side to the other of a poised position without which there can be no vibration.

We shall see that, for the pranic energy, perfect equilibrium between the inspiring and expiring breaths is achieved through the "equinox"[8] practice—and that the poised state of *vīrya*, which draws its potency from the vibration, lies at the junction between pure and impure, or also between excitation and relaxation of the sexual rhythm in the heroic being (*vīra*).[9]

Thus, behind all the rhythms of life is one and the same vibration pervading the body and the universe, one and the same power reverberating upon every level, from the highest mystical power experienced in the form of *spanda* to ordinary virility.

The experience of Kuṇḍalinī is a turning inward and an attunement of all the energies in order to recapture the primordial rhythm; it makes one aware that the passage from duality to unity, from one rhythm to another, is realized through the growing fire of effervescence caught in its first stirring, but without a break and always according to the same process of emission and withdrawal.

8. *Viṣuvat* and *haṃsa*, cf. here p. 89.
9. Cf. here p. 157 and seq.

Our study, then, observes the same scheme, recurring again and again like a leitmotiv on every level of life; while it lends a certain monotony to the exposition, it emphasizes the universal significance of this process based on vibration.

At every stage, the balance of the two opposite movements of a rhythm harmonizes the corresponding energy which becomes one and vibrant. The churned energy, beginning to tremble, rises back to the place of its stirring, the peaceful center from which appear the various aspects of a unifying friction, and similarly Śiva and Śakti, whose bond is indissoluble, part from each other so as to unite once more and to become one: the heart *bindu*.

Two extreme points (the points of the *visarga*) express this twin movement of separation and return, whereas the *bindu* represents the single point from which they emerge and into which they return—the place of unity and power, the place of adamantine intensity, that of Consciousness.

As early as the *Ṛg Veda*, it is from the rubbing of two wooden sticks, the *araṇī*, that the sacrificial fire springs forth. Later, with the Śaivāgama, the great sacrifice is the offering of the Self, an oblation poured into the fire of the supreme conscious Subject, which consumes all limitations.

Part One

AWAKENING AND UNFOLDING OF *KUṆḌALINĪ*

Serpent of the Depths

As such a name implies, the "curled one" with a sinuous body, when lying coiled and dormant in the body, may be compared to a snake. Just as the snake, an object of dread because of its poison, stands as a symbol of all evil forces, as long as she lies motionless within us, Kuṇḍalinī is related to our obscure, unconscious energies, both poisoned and poisonous. However, once they are awakened and under control, these same energies become effective and confer a true power.

Kuṇḍalinī resembles a snake also in the way that she emits her venom. When it wants to bite, the serpent swings around, forming a circle with its tail for a support. Once it stands erect it is no longer dangerous at all. In the same way, as soon as Kuṇḍalinī uncoils and rises—straight like a staff—to the top of the head, not only does she become harmless, but as the evil nature of her power is transformed, she proves to be a priceless treasure.

When all the effects of the poison have been eliminated, glory and power begin to permeate the whole body, as expressed by the term *viṣa*, with its double meaning: pervasive "poison" bringing about death, and also "all-pervasiveness,"[1] that of the nectar of immortality (*amṛta*).

How can the poison of mundane energies be made to serve higher aims? Two solutions are offered: either to digest the poison or to keep the nectar in store under one's control. Is this not the underlying meaning of the myth of Śiva who, out of mercy, drinks the poison extracted from the ocean of milk—the wealth of which he gave out to the gods—and keeps it in his throat which has

1. Cf. here p. 52.

turned a dark blue. Similarly, the yogin with purified body holds in store what has been transformed into divine nectar; in order to pour it forth, he draws from this receptacle of ambrosia which, like the ocean, never increases nor decreases.

Thus Kuṇḍalinī appears as a reservoir of energy, either when remaining concealed in the human body or when, regaining her conscious essence, she vitalizes the tendencies and directs them toward the universal. In this way she becomes a basis for the manifold techniques of yoga and for the highest mystical experiences.

But as a serpent and guardian of the greatest of all treasures—immortality—Kuṇḍalinī calls to mind the ancient serpent of the depths, Ahirbudhnya,[2] celebrated in the Vedas. This serpent is invoked for obtaining food and vigor, at the same time as the earth, the heaven, the ocean, and the promoters of the cosmic pattern (*ṛta*). Its cult is associated with the worship of the most ancient divinities like Aditi ("loosening personified"), mother of the *āditya*, as well as with the worship of the *asura*, guardians of the treasures. Among these divinities, the mysterious serpent of the abyss is very often invoked with Aja-ekapād, the one-footed Unborn, from whom probably it does not differ.

The depths of its realm are those of the ocean, of the atmosphere with its clouds and mists, as well as the depths of the earth out of which surge the beneficient sources; Ahirbudhnya then encircles the universe, enveloping it within itself.

During a vedic ritual the sacrificial seat of the brahmin priest, endowed with "unfathomable knowledge," is thus addressed: "Thou art an all-encompassing ocean, thou art the one-footed unborn, thou art the serpent of the oceanic depths."[3]

Poets and mystics (*kavi* and *ṛṣi*) kept the science related to these ancient divinities so secret that its key was lost, even at the time of the *Ṛg Veda*. As early as that era, the warlike god, drinker of *soma*, Indra, overthrows Asura and Āditya, robs them of the treasure they were jealously guarding and gives it out to his worshippers. At the same time, the serpent Ahi, guardian of the

2. *Budhna*, bottom, base and depth; according to the *Nirukta*, this term refers also to the body. *Budhnya*, which dwells at the base or which comes from the depths—depths of the atmosphere containing the waters, just as the body (*budhna*) contains the breaths.

3. *Yājur Veda*, V.33. Cf. Hymn VI.50.14 of the *Ṛg Veda*, with the commentary by the *Nirukta*, ch. XII.33, cf. also X.44.

sources, becomes a dragon and is defeated by Indra and his attendants.[4]

Again may we not discern some allusion to Kuṇḍalinī in certain myths of ancient India, where the *nāga*, those mighty divinities in the likeness of cobras, play an important role?

In the epic lore we see Viṣṇu asleep in the midst of the primal waters, resting on the manifold coils of the cosmic serpent Ādiśeṣa, also named Ananta, the infinite. It is he who encircles and upholds the earth.

Let us also mention, in probably pre-Aryan India, and especially in Kashmir, the cult of the prestigious *nāga*, both divine serpents and mystic sages, in possession of an eminent science of an occult nature, concealing a heavenly ambrosia.

The serpent divinities are also to be found in many Buddhist legends narrated in the Pālī *Tripiṭaka*; there one sees the Buddha subduing dangerous *nāga*, like the one of Uruvilvā: both fight during a whole night with the blazing fire (*tejas*) they are emitting as their sole weapon; the *nāga*, spitting out its flames, is finally overcome by the fiery splendor of the Buddha. But usually, the *nāga* is won over by the word of the Awakened One and lends him his support. Such is the king of the *nāga*, Muchilinda, who is represented in numerous sculptures standing erect behind the Buddha protecting his head from the elements by spreading his hood like a canopy or sunshade.

However, what allows us to mention the mythic serpent in relation to Kuṇḍalinī is the adoption of this symbol within the Śaiva system itself. As we shall see, in the highest of the initiations by piercing, that which is precisely called "of the serpent" (*bhujaṅgavedha*),[5] the energy ascends with lightning speed to the top of the head and blossoms into bliss in the form of a fivefold-hooded cobra intensely vibrating with life. Thus outstretched above the head, he symbolizes the cosmic *dvādaśānta*; all of the yogin's energies, at this stage, are all-pervading and spread out to the entire universe.

4. In Hemachandra's *Koṣa*, Ahirbudhnya is the name of Śiva himself.
5. Cf. T.A. XXIX 248-251. Cf. here p. 97.

Chapter One

Śiva's Triple Emission and the Three Aspects of Kuṇḍalinī

In the third chapter of the *Tantrāloka*, Abhinavagupta describes the phases of the universal emission in relation to the various aspects of Kuṇḍalinī.

"The supreme energy of the Deity, the *akula*, is [the energy] *kaulikī*, through whom the supreme Consciousness, or *kula*, expands.

The Lord is inseparable from her" (67).

Jayaratha glosses: *Kula*, the supreme Consciousness whence arises the diversified universe and whither it withdraws, is free of Śiva and his energy. This is *anuttara (A)*, the ineffable, pure light and ultimate Reality, giving birth within itself to the essence of the couple Śiva-Śakti when, out of its absolute freedom, it wishes to manifest the universe.

Akula, on the other hand, characterizes Śiva as light (*prakāśa*), transcendent, and unequalled (*anuttara*).

He becomes emitting through his *kaulikī* energy, namely "self-awareness (*vimarśa*)." That supreme subtle energy, Kuṇḍalinī, joins with Śiva in a unifying friction of mutual delight, and then rises and assumes the form of the energies of will, knowledge and activity (p. 17).

"The merging, that of the couple (*yāmala*) Śiva and Śakti, is the energy of bliss (*ānandaśakti, Ā*) wherefrom the entire universe comes into being: a reality beyond the supreme and the nonsupreme, it is called Goddess, essence and (glorious) Heart: this is the emission, the supreme Lord" (68-69).

According to the gloss, the unifying friction is a surging forth, a vibration, a blissful energy originating the universal flow. At this stage Śiva and the energy appear to be distinct: Śiva is transcendent in relation to the universe, while the energy remains immanent, without her plenitude being diminished.

So *kaulikī* is a wish to emit, an awareness, forever one with the supreme conscious Subject. As the effervescence[1] incites a move outward, she starts emitting. Then bliss awakens gradually as the surging forth of the Self is revealed and extends as far as the energy of activity.[2]

The absolute energy, identical with eminent Consciousness (*parasamvit*), is also called *amākalā*, the seventeenth energy, supreme bliss, self-awareness, and complete freedom. Without her nothing would exist. Identical with Śiva, she manifests as Life and universal glory.

Abhinavagupta quotes from the *Triśirobhairava* about this: "The seventeenth *kalā* has ambrosia (*amṛta*) for her essence and mode. Spreading through the movement of the point (*bindu*), which becomes twofold as a supreme-non-supreme emission, she constitutes the manifested effulgence of all things.

"When she does not emit, Kuṇḍalinī assumes the form of pure, quiescent energy, *śaktikuṇḍalikā*. Subsequently she becomes *prāṇakuṇḍalinī*, vital or breath energy. Even when she has reached the extreme point of emission, she remains supreme Kuṇḍalinī, called supreme Brahman, firmament of Śiva and abode of the Self. The alternate movements of emanation and resorption are solely the emission of the Lord."[3]

In quoting from the same Tantra, Jayaratha glosses: the abode of the Self transcending all the ways is called "energy, *kuṇḍalī*, supreme firmament of Consciousness"; undifferentiated, unparalleled, it is beyond the scope of the criteria of knowledge. In this supreme realm, at the peak of the firmament of Conscious-

1. *Procchalantī sthiti.*
2. Comm. of śl.136-137, p. 138-140.
3. III. śl.137-141.

ness, things or notions never arise. Let this highest peak be regarded as the firmament of Śiva, the universal receptacle. As that which grows and makes grow while turned inward, thus appears the supreme Brahman, qualifying everything but not qualified by anything.[4]

Sovereign Consciousness encompasses the movements of emanation and of resorption of the universe in the aspects of knower, knowledge and known, all this being nothing but the Lord's emission.

The Triple Emission (*visarga*)

The term *visarga* refers both to the creative emission (*visṛj-*) and the two points, a mark of the alphabet indicating a slight aspiration at the end of a vowel. Creative emission takes place through a double movement: the unifying friction of Śiva and the energy. In humans also this same movement takes place, in the friction of inhaled and exhaled breaths within the median channel or, as well, in sexual union.

So, *visarga* is the origin and consummation of the flow of virile capacity (*vīrya*) and of Kuṇḍalinī's ascent.

Supreme Emission

Abhinavagupta defines the emitting state (*vaisargikī sthiti*), which is bliss, as "the projection of the Self into the Self and by the Self" (141).

According to Jayaratha, this pure emission of the Lord in which everything proceeds from the Self is a dazzling unfoldment (*parisphūraṇa*) that assumes inner and outer aspects.

Intermediate Emission

Simultaneously supreme and nonsupreme, the emission peculiar to *śaktikuṇḍalinī* pertains to the *kula* energy or *śaktivisarga*. It is Kuṇḍalinī as consciousness (*vimarśakuṇḍalinī*).

The initial movement prior to the actual emission is when

4. Comm. pp. 140-143.

kulakuṇḍalinī begins to stir; she is said to be "swollen"[5] like a seed about to germinate. Pure quiescent energy, *śaktikuṇḍalinī*, not turned outward yet, lies dormant and rests within herself in the form of consciousness (*samvit*). Although free from any emitting flow, she is characterized as *visarjanīya*, because a subtle tendency can be traced in her toward the emission of the universe. It appears as some stirring but still immersed in undivided plenitude, that of perfect interiority, the objective energy being absorbed in and merged with the subjective energy. The single point, *bindu*[6] or *akula* Śiva, starts fissuring, which gives rise to the two points of the *visarga*.

In *śaktikuṇḍalinī* these two points balance perfectly, but should they start to become unbalanced, one predominating over the other, a faint tendency to manifest appears. As soon as one of the points withdraws, the other one becomes visible. If the energy makes the universe arise, Śiva remains unrevealed and without equal; if she resorbs the universe, Śiva shines forth in all his glory. Still the immutable Śiva is never subject to any alteration.

Because of this double point, *śaktikuṇḍalinī* is expressed as the *visarga*, namely the phoneme *Ḥ*, free from manifestation and transcribed in the form of two superposed dots representing the twofold tendency peculiar to this energy:

Ā, bliss (*ānanda*) and *H*, the expression of the act of emitting which ends in vital rhythm or breath (*prāṇa*).

Śiva, bindu, akula = अ

śaktikuṇḍalinī = अः → *parakuṇḍalinī A*
→ *prāṇakuṇḍalinī H*

Since *śaktikuṇḍalinī* participates in the level characterized as both supreme and non-supreme, she is intermediate between the two Kuṇḍalinī described as follows: if her point is turned inward (*āntarkoṭi*), she merges into Śiva and regains her essence as the seventeenth *kalā*, pure consciousness or supreme Kuṇḍalinī. If her point is turned outward and she begins to stir (*kṣobha*), she becomes, at the lower stage of emission, *H*, the energy of vital

5. *Ucchūnantī.*

6. *Anusvāra,* nasal resonance indicated by a point above a consonant symbolizing the condensed energy of speech.

breath, *prāṇakuṇḍalinī*; and, this emission getting more dense, the breath is called *haṃsa* (swan), a consonant.[7]

Lower Emission and *Prāṇakuṇḍalinī*

The Kuṇḍalinī of vital breath precedes the emanation itself, from which emerge the levels of reality (*tattva*).

Situated at the dawn of the cosmic unfoldment, she is still only the first throb of the objective manifestation, a mere tendency to exteriorize, hence the expression "*ādikoṭi*"—point turned toward the origin, namely, the manifestation of the universe.

Kṣemarāja[8] shows how Consciousness transforms itself into vital energy. Although it is the innermost Reality and the universal substratum, the supreme Consciousness, concealing its true essence at the stage of illusion (*māyā*), keeps on exteriorizing, and when it reaches the point (the *bindu* in *H*), its movement comes to an end; then it has unfolded itself into *prāṇa*, as expressed by the famous statement: "Initially Consciousness unfolded itself into vital breath."[9]

Having made vital energy (*prāṇaśakti*) its own during a gradual descent, Consciousness rests at the stages of intelligence, body, etc., following the course of thousands of channels (*nāḍī*). Then it assumes the aspect of the central channel[10] when, taking breath energy for support, it descends from the crown of the head to the lower opening at the base of the spine.[11] It is compared to the central vein of the leaf of the *dhāka* or *palāśa* tree, to which the other ribs connect, for it is from this channel that all functions spring forth, and also within it that they come to rest. This channel is empty (*śūnya*) and it is named *haṃsa*, swan or central breath.[12] In this way, it not only corresponds to the manifestation of the energy, but also to its return to the vital, phonic and cosmic source.

7. Cf.III p. 142 and śl 142.
8. Cf. P.H. sūtra 1, comm.
9. *Prāk samvit prāṇa pariṇatā.* T.A. VI.8 quoting Kallaṭa.
10. *Suṣumnā* or *madhyanāḍī.*
11. From the *brahmarandhra* to the *adhovaktra*.
12. Cf. here p. 49, the enunciation of *OṂ* as spontaneous and eternal movement. According to the S.S.v. III.27, simply breathing means continuous repetition of the breath mantra, viz. *haṃsa*.

Parā or *Pūrṇākuṇḍalinī*

However, in a move toward her origin, Kuṇḍalinī, after having become *śaktikuṇḍalinī*, then *prāṇakuṇḍalinī*, spontaneously returns to plenitude though not deprived of the emitting tendency for, in such plenitude,[13] there is nothing but act and movement; the entire universe, inseparable from Śiva, abides in the supreme energy, *parakuṇḍalinī*.

It is to be noted that this return is an enrichment in comparison to the point of departure, since Kuṇḍalinī then encompasses the whole world. For Śiva to reveal himself as Paramaśiva, the All, beyond immanence and transcendence, Kuṇḍalinī must emerge from him and return to him.

Thus in the Kula system Kuṇḍalinī is regarded as the origin,the substance and the consummation of everything.

13. That of the absolute I (*pūrṇāhantā*) where Śiva and Śakti are inseparably united. Triple *visarga*: *(1)Paravisarga: vaisargikā sthiti, Śiva, akula, bindu, prakāśa = śaktivimarśa; (2) Parāparavisarga: śaktivisarga, śaktikuṇḍalinī, Ḥ, vimarśakuṇḍalinī. visarjanīya* and *kulakuṇḍalinī; (3) Aparavisarga: prāṇakuṇḍalinī, Ḥ, haṃsa*, vital breath.

Chapter Two

The "Coiled" *Kuṇḍalinī* Within the Body

Centers and Nāḍī

Before describing the important stages of Kuṇḍalinī's ascent, it is essential to give some account of the "physiology" of yoga.

Our texts do not elaborate on this matter and we are unwilling to resort to the later treatises of *haṭhayoga*, where the term *cakra* refers to stations or lotuses (*pīṭha* and *padma*), with varying number of petals and respective letters, also described in the latest tantra and Upaniṣad.

Rather than picturesque representations used as a basis for concentration, the *cakra* or wheels are, for the Śaivites of Kashmir, vibratory centers known to them through experience. During the rising of Kuṇḍalinī, since the yogin experiences a vigorous whirling at the level of the centers located along the central axis, the latter are called "whirling wheels." From there the divine energies spread out and become active in the body.[1] Each wheel has a definite number of spokes; fifty in all have been listed for the whole body. These spokes, symbols of a radiant and vibrating energy, subsequently became, in the yogic and tantric systems,

1. Cf. V.36.

petals correlated with inscribed letters, with specific sounds, forms, colors, and functions.

Instead of the seven wheels of those systems, the Trika acknowledges only five main wheels, placed one above the other, from the root center (*mūlādhāra*) to the crown of the head (*brahmarandhra*, the orifice of Brahman).

Between each center is a space the size of three hands' breadth or three superimposed fists. The centers are interconnected by *nāḍī*,[2] subtle currents of vital energy (*prāṇaśakti*). These flux of energies, starting from the centers and permeating the whole body, are said to be 72,000 in number, among which three stand out as the most significant, namely *iḍā, piṅgalā*, and *suṣumnā*. The former two are located respectively to the left and to the right of the median channel, *suṣumnā*, the royal, central way, also called *madhyanāḍī*.

As delicate as the lotus fiber, this road is the divine fiery way along which Kuṇḍalinī ascends to the summit; being empty, it does not offer any obstruction, for it is only in the void that the breath vibrates and becomes conscious again, thus recovering its universal essence.

All along this *nāḍī* there are centers, placed one above the other, which the Kuṇḍalinī has to pierce during her ascent.

In ordinary persons these wheels neither revolve nor vibrate, they form inextricable tangles of coils, called accordingly "knots" (*granthi*), because they "knot" spirit and matter, thus strengthening the sense of ego. Some of these knots of energy, *mūlādhāra* and *bhrū,* are not easily loosened. Together they consitute the unconscious complexes (*saṃskāra*) woven by illusion, and the weight and rigidity of the past offers a strong opposition to the passage of the spiritual force. Each knot, being an obstruction, must be loosened so that the energy released by the centers can be absorbed by Kuṇḍalinī and thus regain its universality.

These wheels are by no means physiological and static centers of the gross body, but centers of power belonging to the subtle body, centers that the yogin alone, during the unfolding of Kuṇḍalinī, can locate with as much accuracy as if they belonged to the body.

2. Strictly speaking, the *nāḍī* is not a static conduit for the circulation of the energy, but a circuit of energetic flux, of vibrant force; nevertheless, we cannot avoid using either the term way, conduit, channel or canal.

Lower Center (*mūlādhāra* or *mūlabhūmi*)

The root support (*mūla*) is located at the junction of the principal energy currents, at the base of the spine. It has two openings which cannot function simultaneously: if one closes, the other opens. Actually, there is only one opening which can be reversed as it were, and it may be likened to a triangle. If its apex is turned downward—hence its name *adhovaktra* (lower opening)[3]—then the spiritual force is dissipated to the benefit of sexual life, as breath and semen follow a downward course. On the contrary, if the yogin overturns the triangle, its apex is thereafter directed upward[4] and the opening called *meḍhrakanda*,[5] at the base of sexual organ, lets in the virile potency which enters the median canal.

This triangle is the *trikoṇa*, "triangular sanctuary," because it is comprised of the three divine energies: will, knowledge, and activity.

It is in the root center that lies, prior to its awakening, the coiled one, inert and unconscious, resembling someone who has absorbed poison. There she is coiled three and a half times round the *bindu*, a point of power which symbolizes Śiva, and the essence of virility (*vīrya*). With her head she blocks access to the median channel. Her sleep is the bondage of the ignorant, making him blindly mistake his body for his true Self. She is then named "receptacle energy" (*ādhāraśakti*), for she contains all the elements of the universe. Although asleep, she is supporting the life of man and of the world, both having fallen into slumber.[6]

Within her coils the sleeping Kuṇḍalinī holds the poison (*viṣa*) which destroys the vitality of human beings, as they dissipate their energies in sexual agitation. But at the time of her arousing, as soon as a pure, perfectly-focused energy reigns supreme, this poison transforms itself into an all-pervading power (*viṣ*),[7] thus opening access to universality.

3. It is also referred to by *janmādhāra*, the base of generation, *janmāgra* and *yonisthāna*.

4. Also named *yoginīvaktra*, mouth of the *yoginī*, *guhyasthāna*, secret seat.

5. *Kanda*, a bulb, is situated five fingers' breadth below the navel and two above the virile member.

6. Cf. S.S.v. II.3 which quotes a long extract from an Āgama.

7. *Viṣ-* in the sense of eating, consuming and also of filling (*vyāpana*). Cf. here p. 15.

Navel Center (*nābhicakra*)

The second wheel, situated in the navel region, is an important center of exchange. From its ten spokes spring forth the ten chief currents (*nāḍī*),[8] ascending pathways having for their main branch the median canal, or *suṣumnā*.

The Heart Center (*hṛdayacakra*)

Inside the third wheel, that of the heart (*hṛdaya*), the energy becomes very subtle. As soon as it is awakened, this center transmits spontaneously its power to the others.[9] Although Kuṇḍalinī may awaken from any of the centers since she is equally present in all of them, it is from the heart that she usually chooses to stir, for, according to Abhinavagupta, the mixing of the breaths and their subsequent merging take place in the heart. When everything has collected there, one enjoys bliss.

Kaṇṭha and *Bhrūmadhya* Centers

The fourth center, *kaṇṭha*,[10] as its name implies, has its seat at the base of the neck or the back of the throat. The fifth center, *bhrūmadhya*, is located between the eyebrows.

There are also, in the upper region of the head, some important points which are not included among the *cakra*: *lalāṭa*, in the middle of the forehead, *tālu* and *triveṇi* on a level with *bhrūmadhya*. *Tālu*, at the back of the vault of the palate, is called as well *lambikā* or *lampikāsthāna*, uvula, and also *catuṣpada*[11] because it sits at the intersection of four ways: those of the ordinary breath, one going down to the lungs and the other rising through the trachea, and the two ways peculiar to the interiorized breath which, blocked in ordinary persons, gives only the yogin access to the

8. They are *iḍā, piṅgalā, suṣumnā, gandhārī, hastijihvā, yaśasvinī, pūṣā, ālambusā, kuhū* and *śaṅkhinī*, as mentioned by Abhinavagupta.

9. When acting exclusively upon it one is safe from a number of accidents and difficulties associated with the awakening of the *mūlādhāra* and the *bhrūmadhya*.

10. The center of purification.

11. The air coagulates here. and as the respiration changes in nature, becoming light, airy, it is a source of peace and pleasure.

suṣumnā: one[12] goes down to the root center and the other, rising to the higher center, is followed by *ūrdhvakuṇḍalinī*. When the energy reaches *tālu*, she is said to generate one thousand rays which radiate down to the shoulder blades.

Triveṇi, a triangle,[13] is found at the confluence of the whole triplicity, fire, sun and moon: *udāna, prāṇa*, and *apāna*. . . .

The subtle center, *bhrūmadhya*, textually "between the eyebrows," presents a particularly difficult passageway for the vital energy. To pass beyond it, one must have mastery over *samādhi* and receive the help of a very good Guru.

Verse 36 of the *Vijñānabhairava* deals with the practice named *bhrūkṣepa* or *bhrūvedha*, the breaking of *bhrū*, which results in the full expansion of the energy. If at that moment the thought is free from duality, transcendence is achieved and one becomes all-pervading. One starts by filling the various centers up to the *bhrūmadhya* with pranic energy, and then, when this center is saturated with concentrated energy and when *samādhi* prevents its dispersion into the outer world, one has only to slightly contract the eyebrows and project this energy immediately upon the narrow dam it has to cross in order to attain the *brahmarandhra*. If one is unable to channel the vital force and send it up toward the crown of the head, the breath dissipates through the nostrils.

Setu is not only a dam holding in check the flow of the inhaled and exhaled breath, but also a bridge linking the center between the eyebrows with the *brahmarandhra*. These two centers, in the ignorant, are always unconnected, whereas in the yogin the vital force, once sublimated, crosses the bridge and reaches *lalāṭa*, in the middle of the forehead. From this state—very rarely attained by a yogin—arises a diffused blissfulness and an intense heat. All functions stop as soon as bliss is enjoyed and the energy spreads inside the head, up to the thousand-spoked center; and since the ties with the *saṃsāra* are broken, she changes into an energy of pure consciousness.

If the term *bindu* is often used to designate the *bhrūmadhya* it is because, when this center is pierced, the pent-up energy that has accumulated there is released, and a dot of dazzling light appears, "a subtle fire flashing forth as a flame." This is the "*bindu*," a dimensionless point—free therefore from duality—in which a maximum of power is concentrated. If the attention is focused

12. Through it *adhaḥkuṇḍalinī* moves to the *mūlādhāra*.
13. About the triangles cf. here pp. 31, 33.

upon it at the moment when, having reached the middle of the forehead, it dissolves, then one is absorbed in the splendor of Consciousness. The three points—the heart *bindu*, the *bindu* between the eyebrows, and the *brahmarandhra bindu*—have then merged into one, as they have been united by Kuṇḍalinī on completion of her ascent.

It is from *bhrū*, and from there only, that the progressive attitude[14] is established with its alternating phases: absorption with closed eyes and absorption with open eyes. At the beginning, when the energy rises to *bhrū*, the breath goes out abruptly through the nose; the eyes open and one inhales; then the eyes close and Kuṇḍalinī, fully erect, manifests as a tremendous flow of powerful energy. When one opens the eyes, the world fills with a new joy which produces intoxication (*ghūrṇi*). When the universal Kuṇḍalinī regains her spontaneous activity, one enjoys the tide of the ocean of life, with its perpetual ebb and flow of emanations and withdrawals. The yogin rests naturally in *unmīlanasamādhi*—absorption-with-open-eyes—and enjoys the highest bliss, *jagadānanda*. To him everything is steeped in bliss, and is nothing but bliss.

In *lalāṭa*, the middle of the forehead, Kuṇḍalinī discovers the entrance of the *brahmarandhra* and her journey comes to an end. From there on the energy becomes supreme and all-pervading.

The *Brahmarandhra* or *Dvādaśānta*

The term *dvādaśānta*, "end of twelve fingers' breadth," refers to three different places. First, externally, it is the exact spot where the ordinary breath dies away, three hands' breadth from the nose. Second, internally, it is the *brahmarandhra*, "orifice or slit of Brahman," at the crown of the skull, at the end of twelve fingers' breadth from the *bhrūmadhya*, following the curve of the head. It belongs to the sole yogin in *samādhi* who has realized the Self, but not Śiva in the universe.[15] The intensely vibrant state of *ghūrṇi* indicates this piercing. Third, above the skull, it is the supreme *dvādaśānta*, twelve fingers' breadth from the *brahma-*

14. *Kramamudrā,* with its two phases, *nimīlana* and *unmīlana samādhi.* Cf. here pp. 64, 76.

15. That is to say *ātmavyāpti* and not yet *śivavyāpti.* Cf. here pp. 59 seq. 167 seq.

randhra, known only by one who has identified with the all-pervading Śiva. It is no longer related to the body; it is the cosmic *dvādaśānta* or *sahasrāra*, a wheel with a thousand spokes, that is to say innumerable energies, resplendent, eternally present, which cannot be attained through any amount of self-effort, for it is the very nature of things (*svābhāvika*).

It is fluid and diffuses the divine nectar, and yet it is as stable as the firmament.[16] Situated above the skull, it consists of the fusion of *bindu* and *nāda*, of Śiva and energy, two identical aspects of the absolute Reality that are light on the one hand and the vibrant resonance on the other.

According to the tradition, the *dvādaśānta* is likened to the circle of the full moon shedding its rays in unbroken waves of beatitude. Inside, a triangle (*triśūla*) of dazzling light represents the triple energy of will, knowledge, and activity. There, the great Void shines gloriously as a subtle *bindu* or *haṃsa*,[17] the very seat of Śiva, free from all illusion and wherein the Self is fully realized.

To lose its natural state of instability, one's thought must be firmly established in this eminent void where all agitation is forever appeased. Therefore, the person who makes the *dvādaśānta* his permanent abode and can lead his energy there at will, attains to liberation while still living.[18]

Suṣumnā, *Cakra* and *Trikoṇa*
Median Way, Wheels and Triangles

The yogin's experiences are illustrated by wheels and triangles. The *cakra* appear to be centers of power where the entire energy first concentrates and then radiates. In this way, all the energies collected in the root center converge toward the navel (*nābhi*) and from there spread, through ten currents, to the upper part of the body. Again the energies converge in the heart and radiate up to the shoulder blades. Finally, gathering at the level

16. Cf. here p. 108.
17. Cf. here p. 23.
18. In the *brahmarandhra* dwells the highest energy in the form of a cosmic wheel containing the levels of reality (*tattva*) extending from the earth to Sadāśiva. From the center of the wheel, where the energy transcending all those levels is united with Śiva, innumerable spokes radiate, and 360 of them illuminate the world, as fire, sun, and moon.

of the throat, they rise on both sides of the head to converge between the eyebrows (*bhrū*), and from there expand to the *brahmarandhra*.

Each wheel includes three additional elements. First, at the periphery, there are the *kalā*, subtle energies to which correspond, at the level of speech, the phonemes or letters (*varṇa* and *mātṛkā*) of the sanskrit alphabet. Second, there are rays that are the *nāda*, vibrant resonances, radiating from the center to the periphery or from the periphery to the center, depending on whether the energy is directed outward or, during the ascension of Kuṇḍalinī, directed inward. Third, at the center of each wheel, the *bindu*, extensionless point, dwells in the *suṣumnā* or median way.

The Kuṇḍalinī practice tends to reunite all the energies of body, thought, and speech in order to blend them into a single current of intense vibrations, which carries them to the center, the *bindu*. Then, melting in the fire of Kuṇḍalinī and becoming *nādānta* (end of sound vibration), the *nāda* converts into an upward flow, the very flow of the *suṣumnā*.[19] The same is repeated in the next center, whose *bindu*, awakened in its turn, joins the *bindu* of the higher center; and this process of unification goes on until there is but one unique *bindu*. The Self, endowed with all its energies harmoniously blended, identifies with Paramaśiva. However, if one of the energies is missing, the yogin, although existing in a state of high spiritual attainment, remains "tied" (*paśu*), for he is not master (*pati*) of all his energies.

Now one can understand how the first and the last letters of the Sanskrit alphabet, *A* and *HA*, constitute the *mātṛkā* and how their merging into one single point, the *bindu*, produces *aham*, the I endowed with plenitude, where Śiva and Śakti, being identical, dissolve into the one Paramaśiva. Hence the particular significance of the great mantra *aham*, the key to the Trika system.

As for the triangle, it is symbolic, in the Trika system, for the triplicity of the energies—fire, sun, and moon—each residing at one of the triangle's summits. They denote respectively knower, knowledge and known, or also the three canals, the three main breaths, and so forth.

Ordinary persons spend their lives swinging between the *iḍā*

19. Such is the inner *kumbhaka*.

and *piṅgalā* channels, between knowledge and known, or the inhaled and exhaled breaths.

In an initial stage *sūrya* and *soma* are merged into *agni*, the fire of the knower, as well as into *suṣumnā*, the median way, and *udāna*, the vertical breath.

Those three, awakened and blended, reach the *bindu* in the center of the triangle, the vital essence that energizes them and enables Kuṇḍalinī to rise. A yogin enjoys the experience of the triangle in *mūlādhāra*, in *bhrūmadhya*, and in the *brahmarandhra*.[20]

In the ordinary course of the breath, there being no *samādhi* state, the lower and upper triangles never meet; nevertheless one may experience a subtle enjoyment of sexual origin, when the breath, going down to the lower center, lightly touches the lower triangle. On the contrary, in a yogin in *samādhi*, whose Kuṇḍalinī is raised, the lower triangle moves up to meet the upper triangle.

As we have seen, at the beginning, in *mūlādhāra*, the point of the lower triangle is naturally directed downward, but when the yogin collects himself, it turns upward. This means that the flow of the *suṣumnā* carries the lower triangle up to *bhrū*, where both triangles turn over and unify. In the *brahmarandhra* they form a six-pointed figure, the *ṣaṭkoṇa*, with the *bindu* as its center, the unique spot for the spontaneous coincidence[21] of Śiva and his energy. This symbol shows how one shifts from one triangle to another without leaving the *ṣaṭkoṇa* formed by their inseparable union.

20. *Trikoṇa, triveṇi,* and *triśūla,* respectively.

21. *Sampuṭa* "encasing," which produces giddiness (*ghūrṇi*), cf. here p. 58.

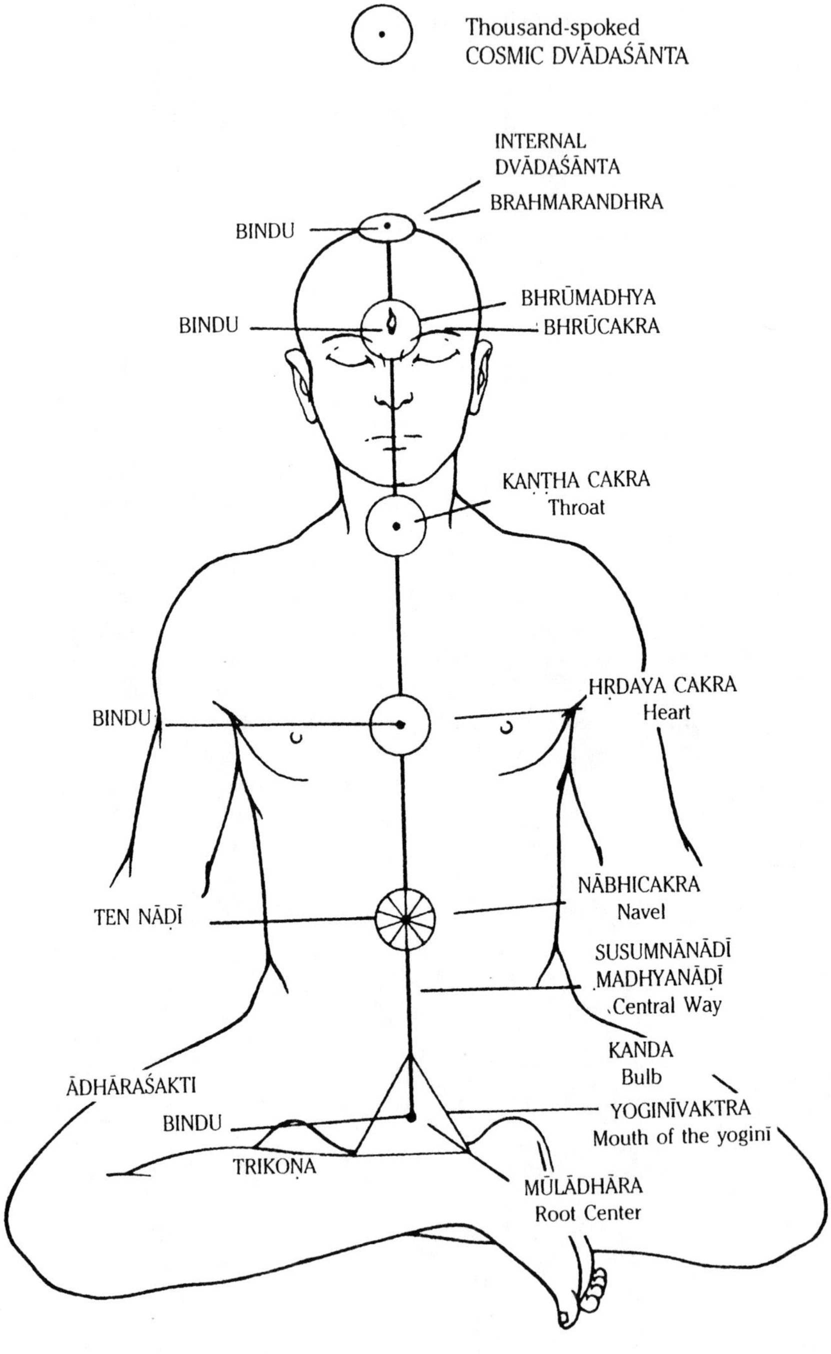
Thousand-spoked
COSMIC DVĀDAŚĀNTA
INTERNAL
DVĀDAŚĀNTA
BRAHMARANDHRA
BINDU
BINDU
BHRŪMADHYA
BHRŪCAKRA
KAṆṬHA CAKRA
Throat
BINDU
HṚDAYA CAKRA
Heart
NĀBHICAKRA
Navel
TEN NĀḌĪ
SUSUMNĀNĀḌĪ
MADHYANĀḌĪ
Central Way
KANDA
Bulb
ĀDHĀRAŚAKTI
YOGINĪVAKTRA
Mouth of the yoginī
BINDU
TRIKOṆA
MŪLĀDHĀRA
Root Center

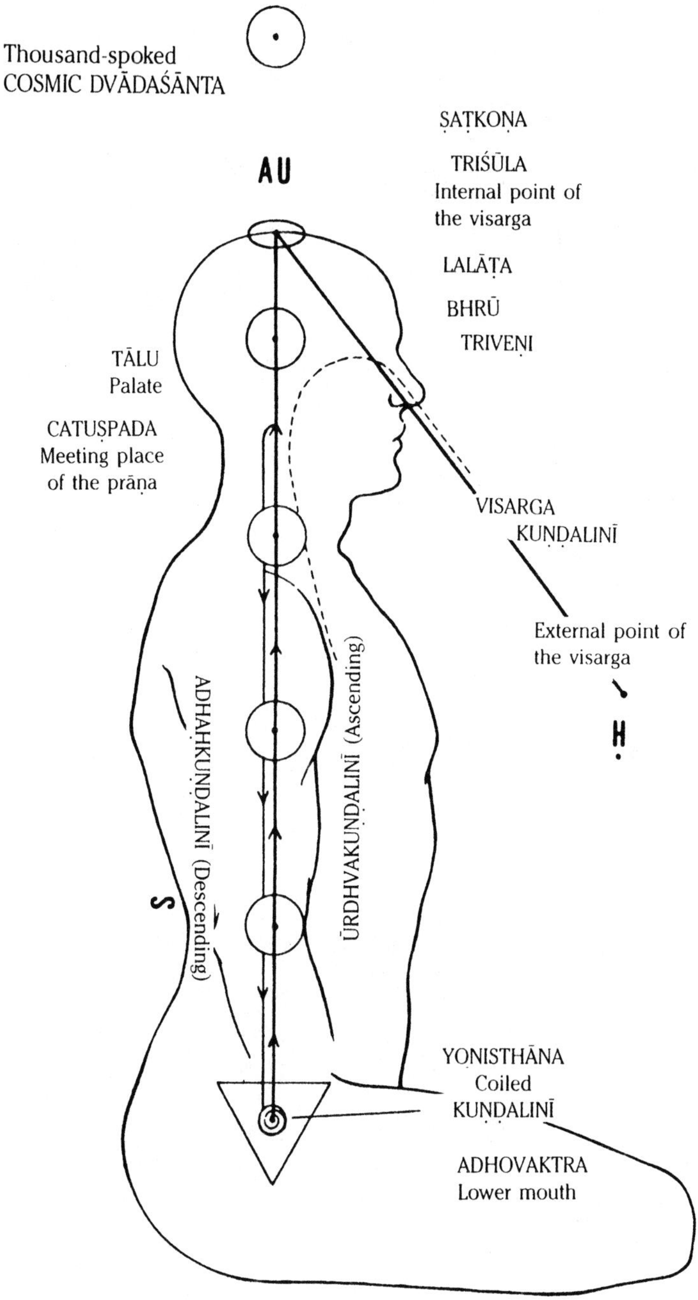
Thousand-spoked
COSMIC DVĀDAŚĀNTA
AU
ṢAṬKOṆA
TRIŚŪLA
Internal point of
the visarga
LALĀṬA
BHRŪ
TRIVEṆI
TĀLU
Palate
CATUṢPADA
Meeting place
of the prāṇa
VISARGA
KUṆḌALINĪ
External point of
the visarga
Ḥ
ADHAḤKUṆḌALINĪ (Descending)
ŪRDHVAKUṆḌALINĪ (Ascending)
S
YOṆISTHĀNA
Coiled
KUṆḌALINĪ
ADHOVAKTRA
Lower mouth

PARABĪJA SAUḤ

Chapter Three

Various Means of Unfolding the Median Way

To arouse the Kuṇḍalinī, concealed within us in a coiled form, some Kaula—worshippers of the energy—do not mind resorting to concrete practices. Their practices, however, have nothing in common with the techniques used by the followers of *haṭhayoga,* for Kaula reject sustained effort, the strong exertion of will-power and the sudden arresting of respiration or seminal discharge.

The true import of the purely inner practices they advocate cannot be grasped unless one knows that each of them puts into play a specific mode of spiritual energy: speech, breath, thought, vibration and various other manifestations of one and the same cosmic power which, under the twofold aspect of the seed-letters (*mātṛkā*) and Kuṇḍalinī, is at work within the human body just as in the emanation and the resorption of the universe.

The Śaiva mystics identify several means to penetrate into the median way, such as the destruction of dichotomized thoughts, the suspension of the inspired and expired breaths, the access to the initial and final extremities of the currents (*nāḍī*), the retraction of the energy into the Self and her unfoldment when she merges into the universe.[1]

1. Abhinavagupta lists them, cf. T.A. 71, p. 377 of Jayaratha's gloss and P.H. sūtra 18. Cf. V.B. p. 37.

1
Vikalpakṣaya, Destruction of Dualizing Thought

One essential condition, the only one really required and to which all the others are subservient, i.e. the destruction of *vikalpa*, is the way of annihilation of all mental duality, of its alternatives and dilemmas. A simple way,[2] it relieves one of such limited disciplines as the internalized exercise of breath and the various attitudes (*mudrā*).

Abhinavagupta writes about this in his gloss to the *Pratyabhijñākārikā* of Utpaladeva (IV.1-11):

> "A yogin whose ordinary consciousness is well collected in the heart and who has no other care, through an awareness free from duality (*avikalpa*) devotes himself entirely to the contemplation of his own consciousness as a conscious Subject liberated from the body and other limitations. And so, ever vigilant, absorbing himself in the Fourth state and in what lies beyond, he puts an end to the dualizing thought and gradually acquires sovereignty."

As soon as the mind calms down and the effervescence ceases, all is appeased and he reaches the supreme state.

2
Means Associated with the Breath (*prāṇa*)

Breath suspension can be produced by certain exercises, which involve holding and lengthening of the respiration, described in a number of Āgama, some emphasizing the stirring up of breaths, others the union of breath with the utterance of sounds (*uccāra*), or as we shall see, various forms of concentration.

To appreciate the full meaning of all these practices, one has to examine the very nature of breath and the prominent place given to it in India.

2. The highest way, known as divine, *śāmbhavopāya*.

The term *prāṇa* or *prāṇaśakti* cannot be translated by any one of the following terms: consciousness, Life, energy, breath, inspiration and expiration. These refer to very distinct concepts, whereas *prāṇa* appears as their common denominator, ranging from conscious universal energy to the very life-force of the body. Thus its nature changes according to the level considered. As soon as it fixes itself in the twin movement of inspiration and expiration, it becomes unconscious, and so do the organs of cognition and the sense organs dependent on it. One is then wholly under their alienating compulsion. And yet, even when unconscious, the breath energy bathes in Consciousness: therefore it can be freed from its automatisms and made more subtle, refined, so that the unconsciousness associated with duality gradually recedes and the life-breath recovers its nature of pure consciousness.

Since *prāṇa* partakes of the life of the body in general (*jīva*), of breath, thought, sense-organs, gaining control over it is to gain control over all of these.

The different practices to this end vary in degrees of subtlety. Set into motion by these practices, the breaths depart from their usual course, in which the exhaled breath (*prāṇa*) starts from the heart[3] and ends twelve fingers' breadth from the nose, while the inhaled breath (*apāna*) moves from the outside to the heart. Should a yogin become aware of these two points of repose and suspend his respiration by maintaining both breaths at their point of origin—the void where they are at rest—then these breaths, interiorizing, become charged with energy and rush into the median way.[4] At this moment, the inspired and expired breaths, usually out of balance,[5] when stabilized at one point and pacified, neutralize each other, balance and merge at the junction, namely in the median way where they disappear in order to give place to the single breath known as "equal" (*samāna*). Within it gathers the vital energy which fills the ten principal *nāḍī*. Having become

3. In fact it starts from the bulb but one is not aware of it.

4. "Let there be exerted an upward push (*uccāra*) on the supreme (energy) formed of two points: expired breath above, inspired breath below, the situation of plenitude arises from their being maintained at the two places of their origin" (V.B. 24).

5. The breath of ordinary humans resides only in *iḍa* and *piṅgalā* and penetrates the *suṣumnā* with difficulty.

the vertical breath (*udāna*),[6] the energy rises, without deviating, as Kuṇḍalinī. When the breath rises spontaneously from the heart to the highest center, it changes into the all-pervading breath (*vyāna*).

Such is the scheme to be kept in mind if one wishes to understand what follows.

Plenitude and vacuity blend into one single experience, for if the yogin abides in undifferentiated plenitude at the junction of the two poles that are the inspired and expired breaths, in the nakedness of the energy, it is because the spontaneous retention of breath goes along with the experience of the void. Accordingly the *Vijñānabhairava*, verse 25, recommends steady practice upon the two voids, at the end of the ingoing and outgoing breaths, as this leads to the discovery of the void in the median way[7] through which the divinized energy unites with Śiva in the highest center, where the wonderful essence reveals itself.

The next verse states:

> If the energy in the form of breath can neither enter nor depart, when it blossoms in the center as free from duality, through it the absolute Essence [is recovered].

For as soon as the fire of *udāna*, internalized and sublimated, dissolves the duality of the *vikalpa*, it assumes the aspect of *vyāna*, cosmic Life, which gives access to the absolute Reality.

6. We will see on p. 139 n.5 that the *Chāndogya Upaniṣad* establishes a correspondance between *udāna* and zenith. In III,10, 2-4, the vibrant form (*kṣobha*) of the Sun is associated to the zenith and to the supreme science, Brahman. And in 11, 1 and 3: "But after having risen in the zenith [the sun] will never rise or set any more. It will sit alone in the center (*madhya*) . . . It neither rises nor sets and once for all it remains in the sky, to him who knows the doctrine of Brahman."

7. In the chapter entitled "About the Middle" (*Granthāvalī*, 31), Kabīr shows the importance of the median void, as it is free of all support: "Kabīr, he who stands in the center (*madhya*) instantly crosses the ocean [of existence] wherein are drowned the worldly-minded attached to both extremes. (1)

"Kabīr, renounce duality and become attached to unity, the former is a source of pain, the latter of comfort. Two means anguish! (2)

"The [fire-]bird builds its nest in the infinite space; it is ever dwelling in the middle—equally remote from earth and sky. Its trust has no support."(3) Hence its free soaring into the boundless void.

Let us also mention in passing other forms of breath suspension, brought about by the utterance of certain phonemes, whether one concentrates exclusively on the initial instant—a very brief emission of the vowel *A*, without nasal resonance or breathing out—or fixes one's mind on the final moment, the *visarga*—a slight aspiration culminating in the void—or else utters a vowel-less consonant; in all those very different cases, a sudden retention of breath may bring about the stilling of discursive thought. As soon as duality comes to an end, what remains is the plenitude of the absolute Sound, a torrent of knowledge, and infinite peace.

Kṣemarāja comments on this in his *Pratyabhijñāhṛdaya*, sūtra 18 and quotes from the *Jñāna-garbha*:

> In one whose mind has been controlled, whose two currents (*nāḍī*) extending on both sides have been stilled by the utterance of a vowel-less phoneme, *K*. . . , in the cave where the heart lotus blooms, blinding darkness is dispelled and the sprout of immaculate Knowledge arises: through it, even in a bound creature, sovereignty may be produced.

Manthana or Churning of the Breaths

Let us now consider how inspiration and expiration disintegrate in the fire of *udāna*.

> The yogin begins by filling his body with breaths which he churns and then holds within; drawing the *prāṇa* naturally flowing upward outside the conduits where it ordinarily moves, he then makes it enter the median canal and brings about the ascension of *apāna* which naturally flows downward. Finally *prāṇa* and *apāna* rise through the central channel.

Abhinavagupta compares the churning of the breaths to that of the sacrificial fire lit by means of two *araṇī*: a wooden stick revolving inside another, hollow one.

> Let the well-collected yogin meditate in his heart on the interplay of *soma*, *sūrya*, and *agni*. Through the friction of the two sticks, from his meditation blazes the fire of the great Bhairava in the form of the vertical breath (*udāna*) which shoots forth in the sacrificial pit of the heart. With this blazing fire, identical with the supreme Subject, he must meditate on knower, knowledge, and known, that is, on the entire triplicity (T.A.V. 22).

Just as the inspired and expired breaths enter the median way, the yogin must concentrate all his might on the fire of consciousness, i.e. the subject full of energy. He interiorizes and then blends the triad of the breaths with that of the energies, whether supreme, nonsupreme, or intermediate.

The two sacrificial sticks correspond to the two points of the *visarga*, which are the energy of bliss (*ānandaśakti*) and the energy of activity displayed in this world (*kriyāśakti*) under its supreme form of vibration (*sphurattā*).

In his commentary on the *Śivasūtra* (II,3), Kṣemarāja mentions certain practices that aim at quickening Kuṇḍalinī by means of air and fire, and through appropriate attitudes. He then cites a passage of the *Tantrasadbhāva* describing in vivid images the awakening of Kuṇḍalinī when churned by the *bindu*, a concentrated point of virile power, symbol of Śiva:

> The subtle and supreme energy sleeps, coiled up in the manner of a snake; she encloses within herself the *bindu* as well as the entire universe, sun, moon, stars, and the different worlds; but she lies senseless, as if stupefied by a poison.
>
> She gets awakened through a profound resonance full of knowledge when she is churned by the *bindu*, Śiva, residing in her. This churning, going on inside the body of Śakti, must be performed with a continuous whirling movement until there appear dazzling sparks (*bindu*) just as the subtle energy [Kuṇḍalinī] rises . . .

The heart *bindu* is Śiva, vitality, power in general and that of the mantra in particular. Kuṇḍalinī is Śakti. From their unifying friction spring forth the various aspects of the sound energy.

To recover her consciousness, the energy has to be, so the text says, "churned with whirling force," *bhramavega—vega*[8] denoting a swift and vibrant movement and *bhrama* a whirl; in other words, a blinding force is necessary here to do away with the dualizing thought and, in this way, recover the original *spanda* freed from the *vikalpa*.

Such a vibration owes its efficiency to its extreme vivacity; moreover it encompasses the totality of an ineffable and undifferentiated energy above all distinction.

Thus the churning goes on impelled by an intense but blind desire, that is, without image or feeling, without attachment to the result, since even a fleeting doubt becomes an obstacle to the awakening of the coiled one.

This churning, we are told, produces sparkles perceptible to the yogin when Kuṇḍalinī rises, with a throb (*nināda*) of pure knowledge, as all distinction between sound and meaning has vanished. The yogin feels life abounding within himself due to the *bindu*, virile power which, present in the coiled up energy, stirs her until she becomes fully erect, and begins her ascent.

Abhinavagupta associates the rising of Kuṇḍalinī to a practice of prolonged respiration (T.A. VII. 3-22) which relies on outer initiation, and yet the superiority of the Trika compared to the similar practices of *haṭhayoga* will become evident. Whereas the latter recommends concentration on the wheels, the Trika advocates concentration only on the breath, since the stimulation of the wheels automatically follows the movement of the purified breath. Just as a peasant watering his field with the help of a noria is only concerned with the oxen that make the wheel rotate and does not worry about the buckets being filled or emptied, in the same way mere concentration on the breath is enough to induce a spontaneous succession of experiences related to the centers, in proportion to the conscious energy running through them. To this end the yogin gradually reduces the number of his respirations by lengthening their duration, and when his breath becomes very subtle, he experiences various sensations in all his centers.

8. *Vij-* found as early as the *Ṛg Veda* (X.18) is a trembling linked to a violent movement, that of the wind for instance.

Although she lived at a later period than that of Abhinavagupta or of Jayaratha, the Kashmirian poetess Lallā praises in vivid images some practices related to breath control and Kuṇḍalinī:[9]

With a rein did I hold back the steed of my thought.
By ardent practice did I bring together the vital airs of my ten *nāḍis*.
Therefore did the digit of the moon melt and descend unto me,
And a void became merged within the Void (69).

The moon of the *brahmarandhra* distils the cool nectar when Kuṇḍalinī, reaching the summit of her ascent, attains the void, the state free from all *vikalpa*.

Verse 37 adds that he who successfully controls inspiration does not feel hunger or thirst any more.

Some obscure stanzas (56-57) allude to the heat experienced by the yogin. Lallā wonders:

Two breathings are there, both taking their rise in the City of the Bulb.
Why then is *hah* cold, and *hāh* hot?

And she answers:

The region of the navel is by nature fiery hot.
Thence proceedeth thy vital air, rising to thy throat, (and issueth from thy mouth as *hāh*).
When it meeteth the river flowing from the *Brahma-randhra* (it issueth from thy mouth as *hah*),
And therefore *hah* is cold, and *hāh* is hot.

9. Lallā's verses are given here in a very fine translation from the Kashmiri: *Lallā-Vākyāni*, or *The Wise Sayings of Lal dĕd*, a mystic poetess of ancient Kashmīr, edited with translation, notes and a vocabulary by Sir George Grierson and Lionel D. Barnett. Published by The Royal Asiatic Society. London, 1920. Asiatic Society Monographs, vol. XVII.

"Vital air" in this translation corresponds to "breath".

Although both breaths, like various other currents, come from the bulb, the exhaled breath is hot while the inhaled breath (*apāna*) is cold. When both breaths happen to meet suddenly, the hot one is cooled, since the moon of the *brahmarandhra* is a source of coolness.

Twice Lallā refers to the bellows handled and controlled by the blacksmith. Like him, the yogin must fill the bellows of his lungs with air while controlling his *prāṇa*:

> Give thou breath to the bellows,
> Even as doth the blacksmith.
> Then will thine iron turn to gold.
> Now it is dawn. Seek thou for the Friend (100).

In verse 4, the bellows is used to light the lamp of adoration and knowledge, and its faint gleam, a purely inner one, fills her whole being:

> Slowly, slowly, did I stop my breath in the bellows-pipe (of my throat).
> Thereby did the lamp (of knowledge) blaze up within me, and then was my true nature revealed unto me.
> I winnowed forth abroad my inner light,
> So that, in the darkness itself, I could seize (the truth) and hold it tight.

In other stanzas she likens daytime to the expired breath and night to the inspired breath:

> The day will be extinguished, and night will come;
> The surface of the earth will become extended to the sky;
> On the day of the new moon, the moon swallowed up the demon of eclipse.
> The illumination of the Self in the organ of thought is the true worship of Śiva (22).

Rāhu, the demon of the eclipse who swallows the sun and the moon, stands for the limited subject, whereas the resplendent moon is the supreme Subject who, staying at the junction of day and night, devours Rāhu there and then. The demon of ignorance who swallowed the nectar of the moon is "eclipsed" in his turn by the supreme Subject whom the moon of the *brahmarandhra* illuminates. Then, as all illusory distinctions and limitations have vanished, heaven and earth become one.

Lallā proclaims in another stanza:

> The steed of my thoughts speedeth over the sky (of my heart).
>
> A hundred thousand leagues traverseth he in the twinkling of an eye.
>
> The wise man knew how to block the wheels (of the chariot) of his outward and inward vital airs, as he seized the horse by the bridle of self-realization (26).

Alternative reading of the last two lines:

> If a man hath not known how to seize the horse by the bridle, the wheels (of the chariot) of his outward and inward vital airs have burst in pieces.

The Syllable *OṂ* and the Synchronization of the Breaths

Lallā advocates a concentration on the center of the navel, with the help of *OṂ*, associated with the rising of Kuṇḍalinī. During the spontaneous breath suspension referred to by the term *sahajakumbhaka*, thought becomes absorbed in Śiva.

> He from whose navel steadfastly proceedeth in its upward course the syllable *ōṃ*, and naught but it,
>
> And for whom the *kumbhaka* exercise formeth a bridge[10] to the *Brahma-randhra*,

10. About this bridge cf. here p. 29 *bhrūkṣepa*. And 'spell' in this stanza translates 'mantra'.

He beareth in his mind the one and only mystic spell,
And of what benefit to him are a thousand spells? (34)

The *praṇava OṂ*, in fact, is endowed with all the virtues contained in the mantras taken as a whole. In stanza 76 Lallā says:

With the help of the *praṇava* Lallā absorbed herself
In union with the Soul-light, and so expelled the fear of death.

She also sings of the supreme potency of *OṂ* upon the breaths:[11]

I locked the doors and windows of my body.
I seized the thief of my vital airs, and controlled my breath.

11. The latest of the early Upaniṣads, *Maitrī*, defines the supreme yoga as the union of everything with the breath and with the syllable *OṂ* (VI.25). The allusion to Kuṇḍalinī is still more evident in verse VI.21:

"The ascending conduit called *suṣumnā* wherein the breath moves, pierces through the vault of the palate (*tālu*); when it combines with the breath, with the syllable *OṂ*, and with the thought, one may rush upward through it.

"If, curling back the tip of the tongue toward the palate and unifying the sense organs, majesty contemplates Majesty, then there is no longer any self. When there is no self, the Absolute stands revealed."

In its final section, the Upaniṣad condenses the essence of its esoteric message, laying emphasis on what has been previously defined as "the space within the heart, the treasure, the bliss and the supreme abode which is our own Self and our *yoga*, and moreover the splendor of fire and sun" (VI,27).

Thus, (in VII,II) we read: "Truly, the essential form of ether (*kha*) in the space of the heart, is the supreme Splendor, with its threefold expression: in fire, sun and breath. The syllable *OṂ* is the essential form of the ether within the space of the heart. Only through it does this Splendor emerge from the abyss, appear, rise, and breathe. In truth, herein lies the everlasting support for meditation upon Brahman. This [Splendor] within the stirring up dwells in the light-radiating heat; it is in the stirring up just like smoke rising in the sky as a great tree, branch after branch. It is like salt thrown into water, like heat in clarified butter or like expansion in one who contemplates. And in this regard it is said: Now, why is it called [like the] flash of lightning? Because, just as it flashes forth, it illuminates the whole body. This is why, with the help of the syllable *OṂ*, this effulgent power should be worshipped."

I bound him tightly in the closet of my heart,
And with the whip of the *praṇava* did I flay him (101).
When by concentration of my thoughts I brought the *praṇava* under my control,
I made my body like a blazing coal.
The six paths I traversed and gained the seventh,
And then did I, Lallā, reach the place of illumination (82).

Lallā identifies *OṂ* with the imperishable and spontaneous sound (*anāhata*) abiding in her heart.

The ever-unobstructed sound, the principle of absolute vacuity, whose abode is the Void,
Which hath no name, nor colour, nor lineage, nor form,
Which they declare to be (successively transformed into) the Sound and the Dot by its own reflection on itself,—
That alone is the god that will mount upon him (15).

Indeed, he awakens when, focussed on the "I", the mantra of silence, he perceives the *bindu*, Siva one with *nāda*, the conscious energy-in-act, which he rules according to his wish.
Lallā again states in stanza 33:

He who hath recognized the *Brahma-randhra* as the shrine of the Self-God,
He who hath known the Unobstructed Sound borne upon the breath (that riseth from the heart) unto the nose,
His vain imaginings of themselves have fled far away,
And he himself (recognizeth) himself as the God. To whom else, therefore, should he offer worship?

Lallā's allusions to the primordial sound and to the syllable *OṂ* can be understood only in the light of ancient Tantra such as the *Svacchanda*. We will examine later on[12] in detail the stages in the purification of the energies, during which breaths, sounds, and vibrations become spontaneously introverted and appeased. Here is a brief outline of the twelve movements of Kuṇḍalinī which correlate with the twelve phonemes from *A* to the *visarga Ḥ*; they move up with the vital breath during the emission of *OṂ*, praised as *haṃsoccāra*, an inner impulse of the breath that infuses life in the body.

The first three stages are concerned with the sounding of the three phonemes *A, U, M*, as Kuṇḍalinī rises through the median way. *A* is the phoneme situated in the heart, *U* is situated in the throat, and *M* at the vault of the palate. The *bindu*, a luminous dot between the eyebrows, on reaching the middle of the forehead, changes into the half-moon (*ardhacandra*); then comes the energy known as the obstructing one (*nirodhikā*) followed by the inner, unsounded resonance (*nāda*), which extends from the middle of the forehead to the crown of the head. As the *nāda* comes to a stop, there arises a still subtler resonance (*nādānta*), which resides in the *brahmarandhra*. Beyond that lies a pure energy (*śakti*), no longer part of the bodily process. The all-pervading energy (*vyāpinī*) follows after. Then, as all bodily limitations have vanished, Kuṇḍalinī fills the whole universe.

With the unperturbed and equal (*samanā*) energy, the preceding stages melt and the ultimate spatiotemporal barriers fall. Accordingly the yogin experiences supernatural powers. The ascent of Kuṇḍalinī is completed as soon as the energy, free from mental conditions (*unmanā*), transcends the preceding eleven motions and becomes one with the perfectly independent energy (*svātantryaśakti*).

3
Contemplation of the Extremities (*koṭinibhālana*)[13]

The initial extremity is the heart, the final extremity the *dvādaśānta*. Through contemplation, individual consciousness is brought to a stop at the very moment when, at one or at the other extremity, breath arises or subsides.

12. Cf. V.B. śl 114, p. 145, Intro., p. 40 and here pp. 57 seq. 201.

13. Cf. T.A.V. śl 71 p. 378 of the comm. on the three extremities, where breath and thought come to rest.

In order to give an example of exercise on the initial extremity, the heart, whence the breath arises, Kṣemarāja quotes from the *Vijñānabhairava*:

> If the senses are annihilated in the ether of the heart and the mind is not attached to anything, one gains access to the center of the well-closed cup of the two lotuses, and acquires the supreme happiness (49).

This verse likens the heart to the chalice of two lotuses with interlaced petals, i.e. knowledge and known. In this innermost space of the heart, ever pure and appeased, reposes the knower, alone, free from knowledge and known.

The final extremity is the *dvādaśānta*, or *brahmarandhra*, upon which the author of the *Vijñānabhairava* recommends to fix one's thought again and again, by all possible means and wherever one might be so that, as restlessness gradually becomes appeased, the Indescribable is attained within a few days (51).

These two extreme points also refer to the extremity of all the bodily conduits which also have to be vitalized by the energy and dilated through various means.

In fact, in its initial or final stage any state of consciousness is free from duality, since it rests in the experience of undifferentiated I-awareness. On the contrary, the intermediate state constitutes the sphere of illusion (*māyā*), within which the I is not apprehended in its plenitude, because it is hidden by objectivity.[14]

4-5
Retraction and Expansion of Energy

Known as *śaktisaṃkocavikāsa*, this subtle practice immediately follows the suspension of the breaths and is used to achieve the full opening of the median way in order to make Kuṇḍalinī enter the heart.

It consists of a twin movement of contraction (*saṃkoca*) and expansion (*vikāsa*) of the energy, which is but one aspect of

14. Cf. M.M. p. 27.

spanda, a form assumed by the imperceptible vibration while becoming manifest as movement.

The retraction of energy into the Self is an interiorization due to a sudden reflux of the energy which, in ordinary life, escapes through the sense organs.

This surging back of all the energies to the center is compared by Kṣemarāja to a frightened tortoise contracting its limbs and drawing them into its shell. He quotes a verse:

> Withdrawn from the outside, one becomes firmly rooted in the ever-present [Self].[15]

There are two kinds of retractions: the first implies some exertion in order to draw together all the subdued energies—breath, speech, thought—and to make them converge one-pointedly in the heart, without the organs ceasing to operate. The second kind of retraction may happen spontaneously in everyday life, whether the dualizing thought process suddenly dissolves or the breath remains suspended owing to a violent emotion such as astonishment, surprise, rage, intense love, terror . . . His energy being thus intensified, the yogin becomes perfectly still, with his consciousness fully collected in a crucial moment, and then he loses the usual awareness of his limited self and of his surroundings. So states the *Vijñānabhairava*:

> If one succeeds in immobilizing his intellect while he is under the sway of desire, anger, greed, illusion, infatuation, envy, then the Reality underlying these [states alone] subsists (101).

Such a retraction of energy is termed "fire," for it consumes duality. It is related to the lower Kuṇḍalinī (*adhaḥkuṇḍalinī*): the breath goes down from the uvula, and as it gradually begins to penetrate into the median way, the yogin enters a *samādhi*-with-closed-eyes.

The unfolding of the energy hidden within is related to *ūrdhvakuṇḍalinī*; it is due to the sudden opening of all the sense organs, when the yogin projects simultaneously all of his sensory

15. P.H. Sūtra 18, comm.

energies toward their respective objects—smells, visions, sounds . . . He remains unmoved at the Center, like the foundation of the world, never losing contact with the inner Reality. Enjoying the *samādhi*-with-open-eyes, he unfolds the cosmos anew and the latter reveals itself in its true essence. Filled with wonder, the yogin recognizes the Self in its universal nature and identifies with Śiva.

The *Vijñānabhairava* shows how he becomes integrated into the whole: fully convinced that he possesses the attributes of the sovereign Śiva—omniscience, omnipresence, and omnipotence—he sings:

> Just as waves arise from water, flames from fire, rays from the sun, in this way the waves of the universe have arisen in differentiated forms from me, the Bhairava (110).

The glory of the manifestation becomes his when he recognizes the identity of the Self, the universe, and Śiva. Such an expansion of energy is called *viṣa*, because the ascending energy, once at the *brahmarandhra*, is then but all-pervasiveness,[16] as the entire universe is permeated by divine energy.

"*Viṣa*," Abhinavagupta writes, "is an all-pervading energy which clouds the luster of what is not all-pervading" (namely *aṇu*, the subject limited by body and thought). And according to the gloss, "*viṣa* is manifested in its reality when the plenitude is revealed at the moment the subject-object division vanishes. Then, from the unifying friction, arises the ambrosian Reality, the starting-point of the unfolding" (T.A. III, 171).

One devotes oneself to retracting and unfolding the energy by means of a practice performed on two different levels: first, expansion and rest concern the lower Kuṇḍalinī, coiled in the root-center: both movements intensify the energy until one feels its penetration at the root, top, and middle of *adhaḥkuṇḍalinī*. To vitalize the breath energy and succeed in realizing the penetration requires a great effort. The second practice aims at contracting and unfolding the higher and ascendant energy, *ūrdhvakuṇḍalinī*,

16. In the manner of poison spreading throughout the body. Cf. here p. 15.

making the energy alternately expand and rest[17] until she stands erect and gradually rises, as soon as the subtle energy has produced the rupture of the center between the eyebrows. This energy appears as a flow of breath which makes the nostrils vibrate.[18]

The text of the *Pratyabhijñāhṛdaya* (sūtra 18), from which I am drawing, is deliberately obscure. The expression "*nāsāpuṭaspandana*" textually denotes the quivering of the nostrils related to a flood of life (*prāṇasaṃcāra*) which differs from *prāṇaśakti* since, at the stage of the raised Kuṇḍalinī, the well-awakened energy blossoms forth[19] and unfolds in the manner of a budding flower.

There are still other methods to intensify the energy and awaken the wheels. All of them are based on vibration and tend to set the subtle energies at work in a yogin's body vibrating. We will not deal with the well-known eight limbs of yoga,[20] but following Kṣemarāja we will mention realizations of a mystical nature, "*bhāvanā* which aim at unfolding the median way and acquiring the bliss of Consciousness. They are revelant only to those who cannot penetrate into the divine essence made of grace" and who must therefore devote themselves to absorption, *samādhi*, also known as *samāveśa*, penetration, fusion, or as *samāpatti*, harmonizing with universal Consciousness.[21]

In this connection Abhinavagupta describes the very significant method known as "the rod practice."

17. *Prasara* (extension, free play), on the one hand, and *viśrānti* (appeasement, resting), on the other. Cf. P.H. Sūtra 18, comm.

18. The nostrils vibrate when the *bhrū* center breaks up. A similar vibration may be experienced in the legs, due, however, to *prabhūśakti*, which is less powerful than *prāṇakuṇḍalinī*.

19. *Unmiṣ-*.

20. For a comparison of their definitions as given in the *Yogasūtra* and those far more profound in the *Netratantra*, cf. *Les Voies de la Mystique ou l'Accès au Sans-accès*, Hermès, nouvelle série, n°1, Editions des Deux Océans, Paris 1981, p. 158 seq.

21. P.H. Sūtra 18, comm.

Chapter Four

The *Parabīja SAUḤ* and the Rod Practice (*prāṇadaṇḍaprayoga*)

SAUḤ is the heart mantra, the supreme I-ness, and it should not be considered as a formula meant for recitation, but as an energy to be activated in order to obtain the comprehension full of potency (*mantravīrya*) through which one goes back to the source—the universal Heart and its rhythm. There the undifferentiated and appeased universe is perceived in its reality as the vibrant heart. 1. *S* for *sat*, which symbolizes the true existence or objectivity (*prameya*), is identical to pure Being.[1] 2. With *AU*, the appeased universe (*śānta*) rises to the stage of the trident of energies on the level of knowledge (*pramāṇa*). It awakens and thus peace is followed by emergence (*udita*). 3. From this pure and intense energy, the universe is emitted (*sṛjate*) within, in the consciousness of Bhairava, the supreme Knower (*pramātṛ*), and thence outwardly; it splits into two points, one above the other, the internal and the external, the *visarga* being endowed with quiescence and emergence (*śāntodita*) as soon as the mantra is realized (*S* + *AU* + *Ḥ*).

1. Therefore this is not the empirical world.

Such is the supreme emitting seed (*parabīja*), a symbol for Bhairava's heart uniting peace and emergence, which unfolds as the universe and allows an all-pervasiveness (*mahāvyāpti*) when, at the moment of the original vibration, the energy, identified with Bhairava's interiorized consciousness, is a mere enjoyment of supreme bliss ambrosia. This immutable bliss, free of space and time limits, is one with the ever-present emission.[2]

In chapter V of the *Tantraloka*,[3] Abhinavagupta describes how the total fusion of the three processes related to breaths, to phonemes—with the mantra *SAUḤ*—and to Kuṇḍalinī's ascent is achieved through the so-called rod-practice.

First, here is the literal translation of the text which I shall seek to elucidate in following Jayaratha's commentary.

> When, with the help of the rod practice, the inspired and expired breaths become even, let the wise one take refuge in the realm of nectar (*S* or *amṛta*)[4] in *lambikā* (uvula), which rests upon a lotus [situated] at the crossroad of the four ways. Having reached the trident stage, where the three channels meet, let him enter the state of equality in *AU*, the melting point of the energies of will, knowledge, and activity.
>
> There, at the stage of *ūrdhvakuṇḍalinī* (raised energy), is found the *visarga, Ḥ*, an emission made of two points adorned by the interiorized vibration.[5] Let the wise one take his rest in this [*visarga*] resembling the stomach of the fish . . .
>
> Just as a she-ass or a mare rejoices in her heart when she enters the sanctuary of pleasure—her innermost dwelling—consisting of expansion and contraction, so let the [yogin] reach the cou-

2. Cf. P.T.v. p. 35.

3. Śl. 54-58. The *uccāra* of the conscious Self is an intense awareness of the mantra linked with the rising movement of Kuṇḍalinī through the median canal.

4. In which the Whole is resplendent.

5. *Udara*; this term is employed elsewhere in reference to the "stomach" of the fish.

> ple made by Bhairava and Bhairavī devoted to unfoldment and retraction, [a couple] from whom overflows the totality of things, ceaselessly emerging from them and withdrawing into them.
>
> In this supreme Heart (the *bīja SAUḤ*), where the great root support *S*, the trident *AU*, and the emission *Ḥ* become one, let him attain rest through universal plenitude (54-61).

This is the place where the supreme Subject enjoys quietude while being filled with all the objects of the universe, whether he resorbs them within himself or manifests them as differentiated.

If vigilance and pure awareness are a great yogin's only requisites for the spontaneous raising of Kuṇḍalinī to occur, the practice utilizing the "rod" of the breaths suits the person who treads the individual path or path of activity. It is named *prāṇadaṇḍaprayoga* because, within a few moments, the Kuṇḍalinī made of breath (*prāṇa*) becomes rigid.

According to a verse quoted by Jayaratha:

> When you strike a snake with a rod, it draws itself up, as stiff as a rod. This is how you must perceive [Kuṇḍalinī] when she is aroused by the Guru.[6]

To draw the vital breath up into the divine way (*suṣumnā* or *viṣuvat*) while avoiding any undulating movement when about to breathe, the yogin turns away from what is internal and external and brings to a stop the oblique (*tiryak*) course of the breath; taking care not to inhale or exhale, he performs in quick succession retractions and expansions with the help of the muscles situated at the *mattagandha* (anus).

The breath, unable to go in or out, stored for a few moments in *lambikā* or *tālu*—a gateway to the median channel—and having thus but a single movement, a single direction, at once becomes stiff. *Tālu* appears as the seat of the life-bestowing nectar,

6. Chap. V, p. 358.

amṛta, or the *S* of the supreme seed *SAUḤ*. Then, when Kuṇḍalinī reaches the sphere of the trident (*triśūlabhūmi*), which is the meeting point of three *nāḍī*, the yogin experiences the energies of will, knowledge, and activity as being balanced. This is *AU* of the mantra, a symbol for the trident.

In other words, the three energies become harmonized in the *brahmarandhra* by passing through the receptacle of the channels—this meeting-point named trident—a blissful domain where the yogin enjoys retraction and expansion of the energy in a wholly spontaneous manner. This state is called "energy of activity in equality" (*kriyāśakti* in *samanā*). Such an activity, independent of any temporal process, appears as the initial stirring of Self-awareness. For the yogin resides at the source of the movements of emanation and resorption of the universe, a state praised as *matsyadarīmata*[7] because it is comparable to the stomach of the fish, which continuously contracts and expands automatically.

This realm of bliss has some connection with sexual experience for, like the *suṣumnā*, the organs are subjected to a similar contraction and expansion conductive to an intimate union which, in a yogin, involves the perfect coincidence of Śiva and the energy, of subject and object, of seed and womb. It is from this coincidence that supreme Beatitude and Consciousness originate.

With *AU*, the yogin repeatedly takes possession of the boundless Kuṇḍalinī whose unfolding progresses in accord with the stages reached by the subtle energies, from *bhrūmadhya* to *samanā*. If at *nādānta* (the end of the resonance) one enters the internal *dvādaśānta*, at the crown of the head, then one experiences *ghūrṇi*,[8] a state of dizziness or reeling, at the moment one shifts from Self-consciousness to universal Consciousness, as the pure energy which has been attained no longer belongs to the centers, for the yogin has transcended the body.

Here three levels of energy are discerned according to whether she is raised (*ūrdhva*), quiet (*śānta*), or perfectly quiet (*praśānta*). The latter is the original aspect of *ūrdhvakuṇḍalinī*, wherein the universe is still unevolved and in seed form.

The all-pervading energy (*vyāpinī*), neither veiled nor limited, manifests in the entire world and corresponds to the sixteenth *kalā* as well as to the great void (*mahāśūnya*). Although

7. Here we can recognize the attitude known as *kramamudrā*, which has become spontaneous. Above p. 30 n. 14.

8. Cf. here pp. 74 seq.

the yogin perceives in it all the worldly activities, he responds to them like one who, absorbed in reading or talking, casually brushes aside the ant which crawls over him, without even stopping his reading or talking.[9]

While in possession of that energy, the yogin enjoys supernatural powers; owing to Kuṇḍalinī who, on completion of her ascent, appears as immanent in the universe, he penetrates into universal Consciousness. At this stage, which yields the fruit of equal energy (*samanā*),[10] all is still, time is no more, for such an energy is far beyond time and space. All the categories of the universe (from the material elements up to the highest levels) have merged into the Self, which is called *ātmavyāpti*, so that the entire universe abides within the Self of the yogin who himself rests in his own Essence. There begins the process of equalization which will culminate in the final stage.

Visarga, Unmanā, and *Kramamudrā*

Beyond description is the highest of the energies, *unmanā*, which transcends thought and its norms, Supreme Heart, Heart of the *yoginī*, enclosing the undifferentiated universe.[11] As the seventeenth *kalā*, it is related to the perfect equilibrium wherein Śiva does not create, although he retains his creative power. There the qualities of omniscience and omnipotence are acquired simultaneously. The final stage is called divine pervasion (*śivavyāpti*): the Self dissolves into Śiva and the latter remains alone on completion of this total fusion termed *mahāvyāpti*.

The *visarga*, as a "flow of bliss" or an emission of the two movements inherent in the harmony between the three energies of the trident, appears as the ever-active *visarga* of the supreme *dvādaśānta*; it contains the movements of retraction and expansion in their entirety and in their simultaneity; without any effort on his part, the yogin then experiences internally as well as externally the withdrawal and unfolding of the energy, thus regaining the coincidence of two extremes; the energies equilibrate on the

9. T.A. XI, com. to śl 30-31.

10. Then the Guru can enter instantly the disciple's consciousness and perform in him what he wishes: open his centers or bring about the rising of Kuṇḍalinī, as we shall see when dealing with *vedhadīkṣā*, here p. 87 seq.

11. T.A.V. 113, p. 422.

three levels: lower center, vault of the palate, and highest center,[12] wherein Kuṇḍalinī completes her ascent.

Abhinavagupta further states in this regard that this emission is embellished in the realm of the raised Kuṇḍalinī when the receptacle of the vibration vibrates simultaneously with the universe enclosed in it; retraction and expansion follow one another spontaneously during *kramamudrā*, and both interior and exterior vibrate together during all activities, so that the two points, squeezed and united by the *bindu*, finally make one.

When this spontaneous movement of alternation has been definitely established, the yogin can go out of or into *samādhi* instantly. Such is the fruit of *ūrdhvakuṇḍalinī* or *visargakuṇḍalinī*, as she is named as soon as she resides in all worldly activities. The nectar of *visarga* is poured into the fire of consciousness and, as the organs recover their full satisfactions, the bliss becomes cosmic. Indeed the universe itself is filled with the nectar of Consciousness which flows through it as well as through us. This is how the *parabīja SAUḤ* works, the union of its three phonemes constituting the unveiled Heart. There the fusion is complete, as the universe has penetrated into the Self and the Self into the universe. Within this Heart, indeed, ultimate and permanent repose is attained.

Since the universe bathes in undifferentiated Consciousness, the yogin experiences the supreme I-ness and discovers the universal Heart as soon as everything is immersed in *ūrdhvakuṇḍalinībhūmi*, nothing henceforward being separate from the conscious light (*prakāśa*).

Technically, as regards the awakening and unfolding of Kuṇḍalinī, there are two theories relative to *SAUḤ*.

First theory

S, the vital energy flows down from *tālu* to the *mūlādhāra* as *adhaḥkuṇḍalinī*.

AU, the energy as *ūrdhvakuṇḍalinī*, rises to the *brahmarandhra*.

Ḥ (*visarga*), Kuṇḍalinī as *visarga* resides in all the activities of the universe. This is the supreme *dvādaśānta*.

12. Namely *mūlādhāra, tālu*, and *brahmarandhra*, where the yogin must discern at once *samatā* and *triśūla*.

Second theory[13]

S, the descent and ascent of the energies, *adhaḥkuṇḍalinī* then *ūrdhvakuṇḍalinī*, the latter containing the energies extending from *nāda* to *samanā* included.

AU, triśūla, harmony of the three energies within the *brahmarandhra* in *samanā*.

The yogin realizes the Self, but not Śiva in the universe.

Ḥ (*visarga*), is *ūrdhvakuṇḍalinībhūmi*, the fruit of *kramamudrāsamatā*, in *unmanā*, the supreme *dvādaśānta*. *Ātmavyāpti* is followed by *śivavyāpti*.

Ūrdhvagaminī, the raised one, is the junction point of the tendency toward creative emission—burst of the energy—on the one hand, and the tendency toward resorption peculiar to Śiva, on the other; the yogin who partakes of it spontaneously gives himself to the divine play of emitting and withdrawing the world.

13. Cf. here pp. 34-35, the diagram.

Chapter Five

Movements of *Kuṇḍalinī* Related to a *Yogin*'s Practice

The supreme Kuṇḍalinī, being the very heart of Śiva, cannot be experienced and thus remains unknown. The great yogin gets at best only a few glimpses of *śaktikuṇḍalinī*. Those forms of Kuṇḍalinī are experienced only after death.[1]

The Kuṇḍalinī of consciousness (*citkuṇḍalinī*) differs from the supreme energy in that she is perceived by a perfectly disinterested and ever-collected yogin.[2] Firmly established at the junction, he is free from all worldly desires: like lightning his vital energy rushes down to the root support—the lower center. The yogin then assumes the attitude of wonder (*cakitāmudrā*), with half-open mouth and wide-open eyes. At once, with a single leap, the fully-awakened Kuṇḍalinī shoots up toward the *brahmarandhra* through the median way. Since she passes quickly through the

1. The yogin is swallowed up by *śaktikuṇḍalinī* at the moment of death.

2. This yogin has not followed any way; he is in *anupāya*.

wheels, they do not vibrate. Although the yogin experiences an intense bliss and is henceforth safe from any falling back into *saṃsāra*, he does not enjoy the bliss peculiar to each center.

Kuṇḍalinī is now as mighty as a tree-trunk, without the help of any practice, not even the one known as the rod. Perfect vigilance alone is enough. The free energy (*svātantrya*), having reached the crown of the head, abides in universal Consciousness and radiates a boundless bliss through the whole being.

This direct rising occurs only in a very advanced yogin, whose Kuṇḍalinī pierces the thousand-spoked center exempt from all movement, thus enabling him to gain access to what lies beyond the fourth state (*turyātīta*).

Such a yogin then is no other than Divine life, Bliss, and true Love.

Prāṇakuṇḍalinī, Breath Energy

Although the highest forms of Kuṇḍalinī are beyond all description, this is not so for the breath Kuṇḍalinī, about whom much information is available and whom it is easier to experience.

She is the one we shall now discuss.

The breath energy rises spontaneously, gradually passing through the various centers, and bestows the supernatural powers related to her. For, while *citkuṇḍalinī* may be said to be pure bliss, *prāṇakuṇḍalinī* is, for her part, pure efficience. As we have seen, she manifests in two successive phases: first as lower Kuṇḍalinī (*adhaḥkuṇḍalinī*), then as *ūrdhvakuṇḍalinī*, known as "raised" or ascendant. The first one is a descent of the energy from the uvula to the root support; she consists in the retraction or interiorization of the energy, in fire and in absorption-with-closed eyes.[3] The second is a rising of the energy through the median channel which she causes to dilate; she corresponds to the unfolding of the energy, to all-pervasiveness, and to absorption-with-open eyes.[4] While the first phase finishes at the threshold of the fourth state (*turya*), the second reaches completion beyond, in *turyātīta*.

These two forms of energy are situated at two different stages of the void: lower Kuṇḍalinī in the void of transition between known and knowledge, while raised Kuṇḍalinī, who per-

3. That is, *saṃkoca, vahni*, and *nimīlanasamādhi*.
4. *Vikāsa, viṣa*, and *unmīlanasamādhi*.

meates the entire body, springs from the void of transition between knowledge and knower.[5] The former is chiefly related to the energy on the level of breathing and of sex, the latter belongs to the cognitive energy, a liberated energy that, no longer bound by thought, is now free to play and, in an open heart, spontaneously ascends to the summit.

Thus it can be understood why such importance is given to the void or emptiness achieved either by suspension of breath or by the disappearance of discursive thought, this being not an inert or unconscious emptiness, but one full of vibration, giving rise to an intense self-awareness.

Adhaḥkuṇḍalinī, Lower Energy

If a yogin merges at the junction of inhaled and exhaled breaths, the breath stops going in or out for half a minute and collects at the back of the throat,[6] then a part of the breath goes out through the nostrils, and another part, spiralling downwards, pierces its way to the median channel into which it rushes, straight down to the base without awakening the centers or making them vibrate; this is why the Kuṇḍalinī thus descending is termed "lower" (*adha*); she is lower not only because of the direction of her course, but owing to the rank she occupies among the various forms of Kuṇḍalinī.

Having become subtle, the energies of the inhaled and exhaled breaths start to operate at the individual level.

Very quiet at first, both breaths unite into an equal breath (*samāna*),[7] central point of unification for the energies. As it awakens the dormant energy within the root support, the equal breath becomes *udāna*, vertical breath, or *ūrdhvakuṇḍalinī*, who rises after having digested the poison, that is, the gross energy.

Ūrdhvakuṇḍalinī, Ascending Energy

The *udāna* breath, therefore, swallows up all duality. In the course of its ascent from wheel to wheel, it is purified as it ap-

5. Cf. *Hymnes aux Kālī*, pp. 27 ff.
6. Which produces a shaking of the head.
7. *Samāna*, which, in the gross body, insures the general balance.

proaches the highest center where it converts into a permeating and all-pervading energy (*vyāna*).[8]

"*Udānaśakti*, surging forth into the median domain, is the fourth state" says Kṣemarāja.[9] According to Abhinavagupta, the rising movement of the vital breath activity "causes all duality to melt away, just like melting butter, and generates a state of oneness. Such is the function of the vertical breath in those who have overcome illusion (*māyā*)."[10]

We have just described the ascent of our free energy (*svātantryaśakti*) under its aspect of raised Kuṇḍalinī, in a great yogin who longs only for the Absolute.

Slow and Gradual Way

However, as long as a yogin is not free from the sense of self, the gradual progression demands a certain preparation:[11] just as one unties a loose and tangled rope before tightening it to make it vibrate, here, one must as it were untie the knots—the blocked centers—in order that Kuṇḍalinī may be free to ascend.

During this ascent through the median way, which lasts about half an hour, each one of the wheels awakens in turn and starts vibrating.

The *Vijñānabhairavatantra* likens this vibration to a tingling sensation as of a crawling ant (*pipīlakā*) and also to an inner resonance:

> When one keeps in check the entire flow [of the sense activities] by means of the breath energy which gradually rises, the moment one feels a tingling sensation, supreme happiness spreads (67).

Rising from the bulb,[12] the vital energy becomes erect and stiff. As the root support starts vibrating, the energy, after a few

8. *Vyāna*, in the ordinary state, permeates the whole body.
9. P.H. p. 6 l. 6
10. I.P.v. II, p. 246 l. 9
11. The latter by no means includes breath exercises (*prāṇāyāma*), for here vigilance and *samādhi* are the only requisites.
12. This is an outgrowth of the subtle body which has nothing in common with the rachidian bulb or any other bulb of the ordinary body.

minutes, reaches the navel wheel; the latter vibrates in its turn, both *cakras* spinning[13] together. Then the wheel of the heart, as soon as it is pierced, moves with the others and the wheel of the throat spins at the same rate as the preceding ones, the whole process generating great heat. It is in the center between the eyebrows that the movement of Kuṇḍalinī comes to an end.

As soon as *bhrū* is pierced, one abides in *citkuṇḍalinī*, conscious energy, where one enjoys the most eminent bliss. But if the center is not pierced, one may at this stage, should a desire arise, display supernatural powers after emerging from *samādhi*. When *adhaḥkuṇḍalinī* changes into *urdhvakuṇḍalinī*, and the conflict between subject and object ceases, one's entire being is overwhelmed by the bliss peculiar to nonduality, the energy being then acutely felt at the root, the middle and the top, as the three are now unified.

The *Vijñānabhairavatantra* devotes several stanzas to Kuṇḍalinī's ascent: "The exhaled breath goes out and the inhaled breath goes in, of their own accord. The one of sinuous form extends. She is the great Goddess, both lower and higher, the supreme Sanctuary." (154)

The breath energy, indeed, is doubly sinuous (*kuṭilākṛti*): when it lies dormant and coiled-up in the root center and also in the inspiration and expiration of any living being, it follows an oblique course, for in ordinary space every movement is oblique; therefore the nasal breath progresses in a curve. But in the true space, there is only verticality.[14] Thus, under the stirring of the breaths as they interiorize and operate in a spontaneous manner, Kuṇḍalinī awakens, stretches out, straightens, and stands erect; when she reaches the highest point of her ascent, uniting with Śiva, she is known as supreme (*parā*).

The great Goddess, then, appears at once as universal Life, energizer of the living beings, and as absolute Consciousness.

The eminent sanctuary, that triangle wherein she dwells bent in her lower aspect and from which she unfolds, is the receptacle of birth, also called "mouth of the *yoginī*." But in her higher aspect, she reaches the triangle[15] that contains the three principal energies harmoniously blended: will, knowledge, and activity.

13. This spinning of the wheels is only to be found in the experiences described by the Śaiva systems of Kaśmir.

14. Here it does not refer to *ākāśa* but to *Kha*, cf. p. 153.

15. Cf. here pp. 32-33, about these two triangles which ultimately become one, forming a six-pointed figure, the *ṣaṭkoṇa*.

As for the true sacrifice, it consists, according to the next verse, in remaining firmly grounded in the rite of great bliss and in carefully focusing on the rising of the energy: then, thanks to the goddess Kuṇḍalinī, into whom one merges deeply, the supreme Bhairava is attained.

In other stanzas of the same tantra two different types of gradual ascent are described, according to whether the energy radiates like beams from the center of each wheel or whether it flashes like lightning.

According to śloka 28, one should concentrate on the breath energy, "resplendent with luminous rays and becoming more and more subtle[16] as she rises from the root center up to the highest center, where, appeased, she dissolves. Such is the awakening, the revelation of Bhairava."

This stanza may refer to the supreme Kuṇḍalinī, who rushes straight to the brain center without taking her rest at every step of the progression, but it may also refer to the indirect way of the breath energy as alleged by Jayaratha, who quotes this same verse to illustrate the indirect ascent of Kuṇḍalinī by successive steps.[17]

The energy becomes more and more subtle as she is interiorized in the course of her ascent. The practice consists of imagining that luminous rays are resorbed into the center of each wheel and penetrate the vertical axis up to the *brahmarandhra*, where they fade into Conscious light (*prakāśa*); the Kuṇḍalinī energy is then fully unfolded and one with the Absolute, Bhairava.

In the next verse, the inner flow of energy no longer radiates like beams, but flashes like lightning. One should then meditate on the vital energy which surges to the crown of the skull, moving "from center to center, step by step, until ultimately the great Awakening [takes place]."[18]

Incomplete or Defective Ways

There exist a number of incomplete courses frequently followed by the Kuṇḍalinī of a yogin who lacks vigilance or even by that of a master when he is busy with worldly tasks.

In these cases, the vital energy moves from *tālu* down to the root center: a part of the breath goes out through the nostrils, and

16. According to the reading of the *Netratantra*.
17. Cf. here p. 63.T.A.V. com. śl 88-89, p. 397.
18. Cf. T.A. comm. p. 401.

another part moves toward the *suṣumnā* and effectuates a partial ascent from the navel to the heart or from the heart to the throat. While the yogin experiences some pleasure and a vivifying ardor—any ascent, even partial, being a source of pleasure and potency—such an ascent should not be regarded as perfect.

Truly defective is the way known as *piśācāveśa*, demoniac penetration. The breath accumulated in *tālu* moves down to *mūlādhāra* without setting it in motion and goes to *bhrūmadhya* which it spins around; it comes back to *tālu*, which begins to vibrate. Then it moves down to the throat, from there to the *nābhi*, and from wheel to wheel down to *mūlādhāra*. Even if the yogin is in *samādhi*, the breath goes out through the nose and the yogin comes back to the ordinary state without deriving any benefit from this practice—neither power nor bliss—for all movement which passes downward through the centers generates either depression, fatigue, or disgust.[19]

19. Cf. *Vedhadīkṣa,* here p. 87.

Chapter Six

Various Reactions Occurring in a *Yogin*

The Five Phases of Vibration or the Signs on the Path

To complete this survey of the various courses of Kuṇḍalinī, the distinctive signs of the different stages will now be described. A vibration of the nostrils, for instance, is indicative of the movement of the breath energy (*prāṇakuṇḍalinī*); however, the passages dealing with all these symptoms are deliberately scattered, and since they belong to different traditions, we cannot present all of our information together. So here we deal exclusively with the basic texts, leaving for subsequent chapters the descriptions given by treatises such as the *Śāktavijñāna* or the *Amaraughaśāsana*.

The *Mālinīvijayatantra* (XI.35) enumerates five major signs of the stages of yoga and of their centers: bliss, giving a jump, trembling, mystical sleep, and whirling (*ghūrṇi*), associated respectively with the lower triangle, the bulb, the heart, the vault of the palate, and the *brahmarandhra*.

Mystical experiences and significant phenomena occur in

rapid succession as the corresponding centers are affected and the Kuṇḍalinī energy begins to spread through the entire being of the yogin. When she saturates the whole body, absolute bliss prevails, but as long as she remains confined to one center, the way is not clear and certain phenomena occur. In fact, the yogin is hardly able to cope with the vibration she generates and each of the centers reacts in its own way. As Abhinavagupta[1] further explains, these experiences are nothing but the reactions of a yogin in contact with plenitude (*pūrṇatāsparśa*).

The reactions hereafter described cease as soon as one becomes identified with Reality.

Ānanda, Bliss

If this contact affects the triangle (*trikoṇa*) known as "mouth of the yoginī" (*yoginīvaktra*), a feeling of bliss is experienced by a yogin who, in spite of his earnest desire to do so, fails to penetrate into the way of the supreme Reality. He has already discovered the interiority of the Self, he dwells in the fourth state, but the bliss flooding through him should not be mistaken for the bliss of the fully-unfolded Kuṇḍalinī, since it is still related to the lower center—*trikoṇa*, or *mūlādhāra*. At this stage, there is only a peaceful state, a self-awareness filled with wonder (*camatkāra*), free of dualizing thought (*vikalpa*). As long as the yogin does not go beyond this modality, he has mastery only over this center and remains there until he gains access to the modalities of the next stage. And indeed the same holds true for the mastery over each of the other centers.

1. Cf. T.A. V.101 ff. The gloss (p. 415) quotes stanzas enumerating ten sucessive states called "trumpeting of the splendor (*tejas*) of the energy." We can recognize there some of our experiences, but they are given in a deliberately erratic order, since enlightening the ignorant who would venture on their own through the treatises must be carefully avoided. They are: trembling (*kampa*), revolving (*bhrama*), whirling (*ghūrṇi*), diving or flight (*plavana*), stability (*sthiratā*), the light of Consciousness (*citprakāśa*), bliss (*ānanda*), celestial vision (*divyadṛṣṭi*), wonder (*camatkṛti*) and lastly, the Indescribable (*avācya*). These ten modalities appear when the supreme category, *Śiva tattva*, is attained. Once this contact has become perfect, there is liberation from the ocean of rebirth.

Udbhava or *Pluti*, Jump or Bound

If the plenitude comes in touch, even lightly and briefly, with the bulb (*kanda*) situated just above the lower center, a certain stirring is experienced and the yogin is startled:[2] this is because, in a flash, he breaks his earthly ties and forgets his body, his ego. Such a jump is due to vibrations that start spreading throughout the body. A yogin who is not yet perfectly interiorized and who does not completely identify with his energy, makes a start. Again he bounds when the energy is forced downward or when she begins moving up by fits and starts.

If there is a continuous immersion in Reality and if one jump is followed by another in quick succession, as Kuṇḍalinī reaches the heart there occurs a violent trembling.

Kampa, Trembling

The false sense of identity with the body, already greatly reduced at the previous stage, grows even fainter during this trembling. The heart center suffers the shock. As soon as it is affected, no objective support remains: the yogin recognizes Consciousness as his own Self and its inherent potency as belonging to the supreme I-ness. At this moment, he breaks the attachment which binds him to the body.

But if, owing to the effect of past impressions accumulated in the course of many births, he has not entirely rejected his sense of identity with the body, he begins to tremble, just like dust on the surface of water as long as it does not really mingle with it. As the body is not pure enough to bear such a vibration, he is seized by an uncontrollable trembling.[3] However, thanks to the joyous assault of the energy giving rise to the subtle trembling that shakes off[4] all limits, the single-pointed yogin loosens the ties by which he was bound to body, thought and ego, as he gradually loses his false impressions.

2. Cf. the *Yogasūtra*'s *udgatha*, when the yogin crosses the boundaries of the bodily sphere.

3. But should the trembling intensify beyond measure, the sense of identification with the body becomes reinforced.

4. Just as one shakes his hands in order to remove a sticky substance that clings to them.

Nidrā, Spiritual Sleep

At this stage the yogin loses consciousness of the objective world. When Kuṇḍalinī reaches the vault of the palate (*tālu*), the yogin feels a kind of drowsiness (*nidrā*) that Saint Theresa of Avila called "the sleep of the powers." Body, will, and knowledge are benumbed but the heart keeps watch. By no means can such a sleep be mistaken for ordinary sleep; the yogin neither sleeps nor dreams, he stands in a special void,[5] his mystical experience is profound, but he is not clearly aware of the fact, for his thought is not operative. The intermediate phase between waking and sleeping should not be confounded with another, lower form of sleep, *yoganidrā*, for it is made up of recollection and subtle vigilance and occurs at a highly-advanced stage in mystical life,[6] when the yogin begins to pour his subjectivity into the universal Consciousness, although he is not yet fit to reside there permanently. Then he stands at the threshold of the next stage into which he cannot yet pass.

Ghūrṇi, Vibrant Whirling

Ghūrṇi is an untranslatable term, for the state it refers to does not belong to ordinary experience: it consists of a specifically mystical whirling, a vibration moving in all directions so intense as to defy the imagination. When its intensity increases to infinity, it becomes one with the ever-active primordial vibration and is none other than the fully-unfolded Kuṇḍalinī in *brahmarandhra*.

Staggering under the effect of his inebriation, the yogin is lifted to universal Consciousness and recognizes his identity with the entire world. Transcending spatio-temporal limits, now all-knowing and all-powerful, he experiences the final pervasion.

On close examination, this whirling, *ghūrṇi*, appears to refer to an inner churning that mixes the two poles of the *kramamudrā*, at the source of emission and resorption.

5. Cf. *Hymnes aux Kālī*, p. 30 and p. 38 on the threefold void: lower void, prior to the attainment of the fourth state; medium void, *samādhi* or conscious *yoganidrā;* and higher void, the sleep of the unrelated Śiva. Such a sleep resembles somewhat the attitude of surprise (*cakitamudrā*): the mouth half opens spontaneously and the breath stands still.

6. Viz. in *śuddhavidyā,* pure Science, and in unrelated Śiva. Cf. here p. 108.

The yogin whose wheels have been pierced one after the other "forcibly" (*haṭhāt*) acquires sovereignty over each of them, and his body, under the influence of Knowledge, is able to accomplish whatever he desires. Prior to this, each wheel had its own bliss over which the yogin had no mastery. But at the stage of *ghūrṇi*, as his energy has turned into the all-pervading *ūrdhva-kuṇḍalinī*, he is present everywhere simultaneously and the indescribable felt in one wheel is now perceived in the others as well. Thus does he deserve the title of "Lord of the wheels" (T.A.V. 108-109). Wherever he goes, all the *cakra* keep humming about him like a swarm of bees surrounding their queen.[7]

Sixfold Upsurge of the Breath and Corresponding Forms of Bliss

Abhinavagupta shows in his *Tantrāloka*[8] how the breaths recover their cosmic nature and he states the seven blisses attendant on this transformation:

1. First, the breath is interiorized at the junction of two states which we will characterize as being similar to twilight, for this is where thought comes to a stop. Thus, between waking and sleeping, or as one awakens and is still drowsy, the inspired and expired breaths rest in the heart and the yogin experiences the first type of bliss which, since it concerns the knower, is called personal (*nijānanda*). As long as the *prāṇāyāma* practice related to the still uninteriorized breath was not relinquished, bliss was only slightly touched upon. But if breath stops completely of its own accord, bringing forth the void free of all objectivity, true bliss, now intimate, is *nijānanda*.

2. It is without any desire for it, without expecting anything, without forming any mental picture that one should take rest in the heart, at the junction of the inspired and expired breaths. This rest lasts for one or two minutes and presently breath, having become subtle, imperceptibly moves outward. Then, suspended and stabilized in the void free of all objectivity, it produces inebriation. Henceforward, bliss is known as complete (*nirānanda*). Motionless, with eyes closed, the yogin loses consciousness of his surroundings.

3. Once outside, the breath, which no longer has anything in common with ordinary breath, enters again in the form of *apāna*

7. Text. like vassals following a universal monarch (T.A. V.30-31).
8. T.A. V.43-53.

and penetrates *tālu*, where it whirls continuously.[9] When it comes to a stop, the lungs being filled with air,[10] one experiences the bliss of inspired breath known as supreme (*parānanda*). Drawn from the objective world, it arises from the fusion of all subjective and objective impressions which, once merged into the Self, vibrate into infinity. The yogin then, enjoying the essence of the Self and free from all desire, stands on the threshold of the fourth state.

4. When, within the median way, the *prāṇa* and *apāna* breaths are balanced in *samāna*, equal breath, the world appears to the yogin as being bathed in equality, with all the forces in it well appeased and in harmony. As breath is suspended, the yogin again takes his rest within himself, in his heart, and identifies with the bliss known as the bliss of Brahman (*brahmānanda*).

The limits between knowledge and known collapse and the breath moves down through the median channel to the root center. Henceforth spontaneity reigns supreme. If the yogin tries to imagine what is going to happen next, he will not go beyond this bliss. Greater love and devotion make it possible to pass through this stage where self-effort, mental concentration, and mantra repetition prove to be utterly fruitless.

5. Breath then swiftly enters the lower center and is nothing but upward soaring: this is the vertical breath (*udāna* or *ūrdhvakuṇḍalinī*), which rises inside the median way, swallowing the whole duality: subject and object, inspiration and expiration, and so on.

The yogin who becomes appeased in the huge flame of *udāna* experiences the great bliss (*mahānanda*) or peace of the pure Subject, where limits and contingencies no longer come to pass.

6. When he rests permanently in this bliss, the fire of *udāna*, which had sprung up within the *suṣumnā* to the *brahmarandhra*, calms down and the diffused breath, Life itself (*vyāna*), surges forth. The yogin experiences the bliss of universal Consciousness (*cidānanda*) peculiar to *citkuṇḍalinī*. And this state of great pervasion (*mahāvyāpti*) is resplendent everywhere, uninterruptedly. No practice whatsoever can lead to this ever-present Consciousness, still enhanced by the supreme ambrosia.[11]

9. Then yawnings and tears of love may occur spontaneously.
10. A phase called *pūraka*.
11. *Nimīlanasamādhi* has given place to *unmīlanasamādhi*.

7. When the breath, with its glorious strength, again goes out and blends with the free energy pervading the universe, the yogin, having acquired the respiration of the liberated-in-life, experiences the bliss known as universal (*jagadānanda*): all-pervading, it surpasses the bliss of Consciousness, for it is related to the total energy at the source of all the breaths, *prāṇaśakti*,[12] which permeates all the creative activities of the supreme conscious Subject. Henceforth the actions performed by a yogin whose all-encompassing heart now pervades the entire universe are of a cosmic nature; he acts upon the world just as an ordinary person acts upon his own body.

12. This is then no longer a matter of breath.

Tantrāloka, V. 100-108, p. 411

Atra bhāvanayā dehagatopāyaiḥ pare pathi ॥ *100*

vivikṣoḥ pūrṇatāsparśāt prāg ānandaḥ prajāyate ।
tato'pi vidyudāpātasadṛśe dehavarjite ॥ *101*

dhāmni kṣaṇaṃ samāveśād udbhavaḥ prasphuṭaṃ plutiḥ ।
jalapāṃsuvad abhyastasaṃviddehaikyahānitaḥ ॥ *102*

svabalākramaṇād dehaśaithilyāt kampam āpnuyāt ।
galite dehatādātmyaniścaye 'ntarmukhatvataḥ ॥ *103*

nidrāyate purā yāvan na rūḍhaḥ saṃvidātmani ।
tataḥ satyapade rūḍho viśvātmatvena saṃvidam ॥ *104*

saṃvidan ghūrṇate ghūrṇir mahāvyāptir yataḥ smṛtā ।
ātmany anātmābhimatau satyām eva hy anātmani ॥ *105*

ātmābhimāno dehādau bandho muktis tu tal layaḥ ।
ādāvanātmanyātmatve līne labdhe nijātmani ॥ *106*

ātmanyanātmatānāśe mahāvyāptiḥ pravartate ।
ānanda udbhavaḥ kampo nindrā ghūrṇiś ca pañcakam ॥ *107*

ity uktam ata eva śrīmālinīvijayottare ।
pradarśite 'sminnānandaprabhṛtau pañcake yadā ॥ *108*

yogī viśet tadā tat tac cakreśatvaṃ haṭhād vrajet ।
yathā sarveśinā bodhenākrāntāpi tanuḥ kvacit । *109*

kiṃcit kartuṃ prabhavati cakṣuṣā rūpasaṃvidam ।
tathaiva cakre kutrāpi praveśāt ko 'pi saṃbhavet ॥ *110*

ānandacakraṃ vahnyaśri kanda udbhava ucyate ।
kampo hṛt tālu nidrā ca ghūrṇiḥ syād ūrdhvakuṇḍalī ॥ *111*

etac ca sphuṭam evoktaṃ śrīmantraśirase mate ।
evaṃ pradarśitoccāraviśrāntihṛdayaṃ param ॥ *112*

yat tad avyaktaliṅgaṃ nṛśivaśaktyavibhāgavat ।
atra viśvam idaṃ līnam atrāntaḥsthaṃ ca gamyate ॥ *113*

Chapter Seven

Cosmic Kuṇḍalinī or the Intimate Sacrifice

To evoke the supreme Kuṇḍalinī, Abhinavagupta unfolds a vast panorama that includes breath, intellect, void, energies, bodily and universal elements: "Let the vital breath, the intellect, and the void be revered," he says, "by perceiving first the identity between them, then their identity with Śiva."[1]

The awakening of the coiled-up energy, achieved through the use of formulas, gives a glimpse into the main phases of its unfolding. *Hrīṃ,* the seed of illusion, awakens the coiled one, the primal energy which lies dormant in the lower center, while other mantra generate the four elements—earth, water, air, and fire—latent therein.

If the awakening of Kuṇḍalinī is thus associated with the appearance of the universal categories, this is because, essentially, the individual body does not differ from the universal body. Thus there is no need to go out of the body to perceive the universal elements; one has only to set up the pillar of knowledge at the very center of all activities to realize that the universe is pervaded by Consciousness.

1. Here we give excerpts from the *Tantrāloka* (XV, śl. 295 ff.) and the *Mālinīvijayatantra* (VIII, 54–76). About this sacrifice performed through *nyāsa,* we refer the reader to André Padoux's doctoral dissertation: "Recherches sur la symbolique de l'énergie de la Parole," p. 358–61, and the diagram, p. 360.

One then imagines a vertical axis called "infinite," *ananta,* extending up to the uvula and containing the levels of reality from the subtle elements to the *kalā* energies. In other words, from the awakened Kuṇḍalinī arises a stem, symbol for the royal road—*suṣumnā*—which goes from the center to *lambikā* and terminates in the *brahmarandhra,* the entire universe assuming the form of a lotus.

At first there arises, through the action of the semivowels, four aspects of the intellect giving birth to duty, knowledge, renunciation, and sovereignty. Then, at the opposite extreme, there arises, through the action of the barren phonemes, four energies.

The intellect is engendered by the power of illusion; the eight energies form a knot, an ocean of ties—the night of illusion. If one fails to cut the knot, union with Śiva[2] is impossible.

Above this knot just below the trident, one should meditate on the pure Science which, extending between *lambikā* and the *brahmarandhra,* contains most of the sense organs.

An upturned lotus, whose twenty-four stamens symbolize the occlusives in identical number, corresponds to the stage of the energy known as equal (*samanā*). The stamens are then turned downward, for Śiva is watching the universe which he rules. They turn upward as soon as the supramental energy reigns supreme. In the petals, the stamen and the center of the lotus, one should meditate upon the divinities saturated with energy: Rudra, Viṣṇu, and Brahma, who govern respectively fire, moon and sun.

At the top, in the *brahmarandhra,* is an eight-petalled lotus, the eight vowels being the eight divine energies; the ninth one, in the center, constitutes Life.[3]

Beyond that, one should imagine the great Departed One, Sadāśiva, laughing and conscious, with resplendent body. From his navel arises a trident (*triśūla*) whose points, representing the lower, intermediate, and higher energies,[4] reach the cosmic *dvādaśānta.* Still higher one should meditate on three shining lotuses composed of the supramental energy (*unmanī*), the universal sovereign. Such is the throne formed by the thirty-seven levels of reality—a worthy object of adoration.

On this throne let Sadāśiva be worshipped as the great Departed One, and above him let there be an offering of flowers and

2. From the M.V. (śl. 57–59).
3. This is *unmanī,* transcending thought.
4. The *śakti, vyāpinī* and *samanā* energies.

perfumes to the supreme goddess, Mātṛsadbhāva, whose mantra is *SAUḤ*. This is Kālasaṃkarṣiṇī[5] who, in an instant, swallows up time. Moreover, this is Consciousness itself, ultimate substratum and absolute freedom.

This vivid exposition means that Sadāśiva has handed over his functions to the Tripūrasundarī energy enthroned at the top of the image. The eternal Śiva, facing upward, flashing forth with innumerable rays, is characterized as the great Departed One (*mahāpreta*), "parted beyond," because of his explosive laugh (*aṭṭahasa*).[6]

The superiority of the Goddess over Sadāśiva, lying motionless at her feet, unconscious of the universe but supremely happy, is that she has perfect self-awareness (*vimarśa*) which is both freedom and power. For his part, Śiva possesses the undifferentiated Consciousness (*prakāśa*) and, while he indeed transcends all the levels of reality, the Goddess is still beyond immanence and transcendence because she is the Whole. So at the ultimate stage of indescribable energy (*unmanī*), Kuṇḍalinī is seated on Śiva while illuminating the universal Consciousness.

5. The one who squeezes time. Cf. *Hymnes aux Kālī*, pp. 11 and 79.
6. M.V. VIII 68.

Part Two

PIERCING OF THE CENTERS AND STAGES OF THE ASCENT

Chapter One

Vedhadīkṣā, Initiation through Penetration

The indescribable transmission from master to disciple takes place from heart to heart, from body to body. Since in reality there exists only one Consciousness—the infinite realm of illumination—one can understand how the master's illumined consciousness is able to penetrate the disciple's obscured consciousness in order to enlighten it.

In two early Upaniṣad, the *Bṛhadāraṇyaka* and the *Kauṣītaki,* there is already a description of *saṃpratti,* a sacrificial ceremony during which a father, at the hour of death, identifies with his son through all the different parts of his body:

"Now, the father-to-son transmission, as it is called. When the father is on the verge of death, he sends for his son. After scattering fresh grass all over the house, setting up the fire and putting by his side a water jug with a cup, the father goes to his bed, donned in a new suit. Then the son comes and lies down on him, with his sense organs touching those [of his father]. Or else [the latter] may perform the transmission when [the son] is sitting in front of him."

Then he performs the transmission: 'I want my voice to be placed in thee,' the father says. 'I receive thy voice in me,' says the son. 'I want my breath to be placed in thee,' the father says. 'I receive thy breath in me,' says the son. [This goes on likewise with sight, hearing, taste, actions, pleasure and pain, procreation, gait, intellect, and the son receives them all. . . .[1]]

The Plenary Oblation

The transmission of breaths from *guru* to disciple calls to mind the Vedic *agnihotra* performed by the householder who, morning and evening, has to pour an oblation of milk and oil into the sacrificial fire, *āhavanīya,* which consumes the ritual oblations and carries them to the gods to appease their hunger. Later with the *Chāndogya Upaniṣad,* this offering to the divinities becomes an offering dedicated to the five breaths, the organs, and their corresponding divinities—that is, the now-satisfied energies. Such a gift should be offered in the mystic fire, the universal Self (*ātman vaiśvānara*),[2] for "he who, understanding this, offers the *agnihotra,* it is in all the worlds, in all beings and in all selves that his offering is made" (V. 19–24).

Many years later, Abhinavagupta gives the Vedic offering a specifically mystical interpretation. While he too calls it "plenary oblation" (*pūrṇahuti*), he acknowledges no other divine fire able to consume the whole duality than Kuṇḍalinī nor any other offering to be poured into this fire than the master's penetration into the breath of the disciple, within whom the divine fire awakens and the flame of Kuṇḍalinī rises.

On several occasions he deals with this theme, one he has at heart. In his *vivaraṇa* to the *Parātriṃśikā*, he shows in what spirit one should perform the sacrifice. The oblation is offered into the sacrificial fire which, fed by each and every thing, internally consumes the seeds of latent impressions (*vāsanā*); it consists in forsaking the limited I through self-surrender which alone gives access to the supreme I-ness, an undivided mass of consciousness and plenitude, namely Śiva and his energy.

This sacrificial fire is no less than the great splendor of the supreme Bhairava, perpetually surging up amidst the *araṇi* of the supreme energy when, stirred up by the profuse outpouring of clarified butter [semen], she is "churned" by the effervescence of the unversal and intense love [-embrace].

1. *Kauṣītaki Upaniṣad,* II.15, translated into French by Louis Renou, p. 46, Ed. Adrien Maisonneuve, Paris 1948.

2. Agni's designation as "all-pervading" (*vaiśvānara*) is henceforth transferred to the Self (*ātman*).

In his gloss to the *Bhagavad Gītā* (IV. 24), Abhinavagupta specifies that the offered substances, such as clarified butter, reach the supreme *brahman*, as It is the very essence of the sacrifice and, by Itself, plenary oblation.

"*Brahman* is the offering, It is the clarified butter (*havis*), and by *brahman* the oblation is poured into the fire which too is *brahman*. In truth *brahman* is to be attained by one who becomes absorbed in the *brahman*-in-act."

Abhinavagupta interprets this stanza as follows: *arpaṇa*, the gift, is the penetration into *brahman* of all that arose from it. *Havis* is the whole universe, and the appeased fire is the supreme Consciousness. As to *brahman*'s oblation: whatever the activity performed by such a sacrificer, the supreme Consciousness reveals itself, as his *samādhi* is a *brahmakarman*, a way leading to the Self and yielding but one fruit, *brahman*, the Absolute.

Penetration of the *Guru* into the Disciple's Breaths

This *pūrṇāhuti* is of primary importance to Abhinavagupta for, he says, "it is by becoming firmly established in this plenary oblation that a master bestows the liberating initiation."[3] This refers to the yogic practice known as "*haṃsa*,"[4] "swan," adopted by a *guru* in order to stir up and enlighten the initiate's consciousness. He first unites his consciousness with the supreme Consciousness; then, infusing his consciousness into the disciple's, he penetrates therein by successive stations, one being known as the equinox (*viṣuvat*), a perfect equality particular to the void where the inspired and expired breaths terminate.

But once again we must turn to his gloss of the *Bhagavad Gītā*, for here he discloses the secrets of the transmission through breath, while giving a fresh interpretation to a verse dealing with the great sacrifice, *svādhyāyayajña*, "the one performed for one's own sake."

"Others offer as sacrifice the expired breath in the inspired, and the inspired breath in the expired; restraining the flow of the expired and inspired breaths, they devote themselves solely to breath control."[5]

3. P. T. v. p. 27.
4. Cf. here p. 10.
5. *Apāne juhvati prāṇam prāṇe pānaṃ tathāpare/prāṇāpānagatī ruddhvā prāṇāyāmaparāyaṇāḥ//* IV.29.

Abhinavagupta explains that the sacrifice is not performed for one's own sake alone, but for the sake of others as well. Thus it is carried out in two steps: first, within one's own self (*svādhyāya*): the expired breath (*prāṇa*) being the resonance (*nāda*) that arises while extending from *A* to the equal energy (*samanā*), namely the *praṇava OṂ* coupled with the rising of Kuṇḍalinī.[6]

The *guru* offers this exhaled breath as an oblation in the inhaled breath, penetrating to the core of his own bliss, and makes this initial massive flow (*piṇḍa*) of *prāṇa* steady and firm, so as to instill it next into his disciple. Such is the first "recitation" for one's own sake or the firmness of the *guru*'s *apāna*.

Then the master enters the disciple's body and, through the medium of the breath, he once again makes the twin offering of *prāṇa* in *apāna* and vice versa.

And this consciousness which has entered his inhaled breath is inserted into the disciple's sound vibration (*nāda*) so that it be purified.

When the exhaled breath is offered in the inhaled breath at the time of internal plenitude (*pūraka*), the *guru* becomes immersed in his own bliss, then he takes in the disciple's impure breath and purifies it. When the inspired breath is offered in the expired breath, that is the external void (*recaka*), the *guru* enters into his disciple, who takes back the breath thus purified. In this way, the *guru*'s *pūraka* becomes the disciple's *recaka* and vice versa, in a continuous back and forth movement. With *pūraka* the enjoyment of sense objects becomes interiorized; with *recaka*, there is an outward movement to allow apprehension of objects.

And again, when the *guru* exhales the breath, from the phoneme *A* to the equal energy, the *śiṣya* takes it back as his inhaled breath, but when it goes out of the disciple this breath is impure and must be taken again by the *guru* to be purified. The *guru* continues thus until the disciple's breath reaches the *brahmarandhra* and the consciousness of each is perfectly still. Then, in a single instant, the *guru* manifests the *praṇava OṂ* in his own essence and, inhaling the breath, he becomes one with the disciple.

This is how the *svādhyāya* sacrifice is performed.

Several points need to be clarified: that exchange of breath is by no means related to the ordinary *prāṇa* and *apāna*, but to their subtle nature, once they have entered into the median way.

6. Cf. here p. 49.

Furthermore, there are two requirements for this sacrifice: the master must be able to release his consciousness from his body to infuse it into the disciple's consciousness; and the latter, for his part, must be prepared to instantly take in the expired breath of the master. Then, filled with the *guru*'s consciousness, he gradually comes to share the various aspects of his blissful state.[7]

The transmission of *mantravīrya* or efficience of the perfectly-controlled conscious energy is a long and difficult practice, especially in the case of the *abhiṣeka*[8] of a disciple who is to become a master himself; since it requires that the initiate be of unfailing faith, steadfastness and dedication, few indeed are those on whom it is bestowed.

According to the *vivaraṇa* to the *Parātriṃśikā* (p. 27), the *guru* inserts his consciousness into that of the disciple at a point called "equinox" (*viṣuvat*), because there the inspired and expired breaths are in equilibrium, equal, and therefore appeased. Abhinavagupta mentions two distinct types of oblation, one partial, if the disciple intends to enjoy worldly pleasures during life and obtain liberation at death, the other total, if he has but one single desire, to unite with Śiva.

Initiations by Piercing of the Centers

Various initiations, performed on a purely inner level by piercing the centers, bring the median breath energy (*madhyaprāṇa-kuṇḍalinī*) into play. They are meant for masters and disciples whose Kuṇḍalinī is awakened. We shall see how the master, by acting on his own Kuṇḍalinī, raises that of the disciple by entering his body through all or any one of the nine apertures, as he chooses.

Abhinavagupta briefly describes these initiations in Chapter 29 (236–253) of the *Tantrāloka:*

> 236. For the benefit of a disciple longing for immediate experience, a *guru* practising a highly efficient yoga can celebrate the initiation-through-

7. Cf. here p. 75.

8. This ceremony was, originally, the enthronement of a prince by a Brahman priest. Here pp. 100 seq.

> piercing that instantly grants him the longed-for fruit.

To define the term *vedha,* penetration or piercing, Jayaratha quotes a verse of unknown authorship according to which the breath energy, acting as a drill, pierces the Self, viewed here as a precious stone. "Such is the type of piercing by which the bonds can be untied" (p. 148).

Due to his proficiency in the practice of Kundalini, such a *guru* differs from a mere scholar; book knowledge remains fruitless if not paralleled with extensive experience.

> 237–238. This initiation by penetration, described here and there in the treatises, and in many ways, should be performed by a master well versed [in this field]. When duly performed, it consists of penetrating higher and higher into the disciple, who clearly and unmistakably feels it through his centers. This is how he acquires supernatural powers. . . . However, according to the *Ratnamālātantra,* if he fails to bring about the rising from wheel to wheel, the penetration then goes downward and will be termed as demoniac.[9]

In a verse quoted by Jayaratha, those two antagonistic movements are clearly indicated: the ascending course bestows liberation and awareness, while the untoward descending course is related to penetration by a demon (p. 249).

Indeed, if instead of moving upward the flow of energy goes down from wheel to wheel, no fruit is born; still worse, this flow becomes an obstacle to spiritual life, leading to depression and a dissipation of energy. Such a process endangers both master and disciple, for the benefits as well as the risks involved in these initiations are shared by both. A failure is due either to the master being not sufficiently experienced or to the disciple not sufficiently prepared.

9. *Piśācāveśa,* cf. here p. 69. Our analysis of the next stanzas draws partly on Jayaratha's gloss.

239–240. In the *Gahvaratantra,* the Lord mentions a sixfold initiation by penetration: [the first four forms] resort to the mystic formula ["I"], to the inner sound, to the *bindu* or virile potency, and to the energy; [the last two], to the serpent penetration and to the supreme penetration.

These penetrations yield much the same results, however, some of them are more complete or more efficient than others.

In all of them the *guru* makes the breath enter into the lower center of his own body and then performs the type of penetration which he deems specially fit for the disciple.

Mantravedha. Piercing of the Centers by Means of Mantra

240–243. The [master] first meditates on the eight-spoked center [that of the heart] . . . , dazzling with light. Then, through it, he penetrates into the heart wheel of his disciple. Such is the penetration by means of mantra ["I"]. Or else, having established the letter Ā[10] in [his own] body in a ninefold way, the master sends it through yogic projection into the disciple's body where, fiery and ablaze, it loosens his bonds, enabling him to unite with the supreme Reality. This method, expounded in the *Dīkṣottaratantra,* was revealed to me by my master Śambhunātha.

The spontaneous mantra, which springs out of the disciple's eagerness to recognize the supreme I-ness, is by no means a sound or a formula, but a realization of the "I" (*aham*) of such overwhelming power that it pierces the heart *cakra.* Thus it appears as a heart-to-heart initiation since through the power of the "I" realized in his own heart, the master touches the heart of his disciple.

10. Or the wheel of Kuṇḍalinī.

Kuṇḍalinī begins to move from the root center. First, the guru prepares the eight-spoked wheel[11] in his own heart, then unfolds it. For, as she moves up to the heart which starts vibrating, Kuṇḍalinī must be full of force and ardor, or else she would not be able to pierce the disciple's heart. Sending her out through the nine apertures of his body, the *guru* makes her enter the initiate's body through the same apertures; then, in the form of the mantra "I," he makes her ascend through all of the centers to the *brahmarandhra.*

Nādavedha, Piercing through Mystic Resonance

> 243–244. Known as *nādavedha*[12] is the piercing brought about by the upward push of the resonance according to the process of creation [of the *mālinī* going from *NA* to *PHA*]; through this spontaneous resonance, let the master enter the disciple's consciousness. This is what is called piercing through mystic resonance.

This type of penetration, meant for a yogin wishing to work for the welfare of the world, is performed through the help of a sustained sound. It is called a creative process because it goes from master to disciple.[13] The inner sound, similar to the sound perceived when the ears are stopped, first arises in the median way of the *guru,* and moves up to his heart or his *brahmarandhra*—as both have now become one. At the same moment it spontaneously enters the body of the disciple, whose breath is converted into resonance, *anacka.*[14] The latter then moves down from the heart to the *mūlādhāra* wheel, which starts spinning; thence it moves back up to the *brahmarandhra,* piercing the wheels which vibrate one after the other, and the disciple becomes aware of the course of this mystic resonance.

11. And thus that of the heart, in preference to the twelve-spoked wheel situated in the navel region (Jayaratha).

12. Here *nāda* is synonymous with *dhvāni* and *anāhata.*

13. By contrast the process of resorption going from disciple to *guru* is not appropriate in the present case.

14. Cf. here p. 41.

The descent of the Kuṇḍalinī resonance from heart to root center should not be confused with the descent of the demoniac way, during which the energy, as it moves down from wheel to wheel, activates them one by one; for here, the descent occurs at the beginning of the practice and prior to the ascent of Kuṇḍalinī from center to center.

Jayaratha quotes three cryptic verses from the "profound" Tantra (the *Gahvara*): "[Let the master], emitting first a sustained sound, take hold of the sound within the sound itself; then, uttering the phonemes from *NA* to *PHA*, let him purify the pathway of the phonemes and perform the piercing by means of sound. That, O Goddess, is what is called 'piercing through sound.'"

Binduvedha. Piercing through Virile Potency

> 244–245. O Maheśānī! Let [the master], whose virile potency (*bindu*) shines forth like a flame, illumine—through its help—the [disciple's] consciousness fixed in the *bindu*'s seat [and already] firmly established on the pathway between the eyebrows; or else, let him pierce the target of his heart; this is what is praised as the so-called penetration of the *bindu* [virile potency].

During this penetration the guru gathers into his heart all his virile potency (*bindu*), brings it to its full force and, when it becomes a live flame capable of enlightening the disciple's consciousness, he takes it up to the middle of his eyebrows; then he makes it enter the consciousness of the disciple, who, likewise, focuses on the *bindu* situated between the eyebrows. If the disciple's center is pure and fully awakened, the master deposits the virile potency there; if not, he places it in his heart, or if again impossible, in the bulb. Then, as it touches the root center, the breath is transformed into a very powerful seminal flow which, in both master and disciple, spreads throughout the body and rises to the *brahmarandhra;* the initiate, then, becomes aware of the virile potency streaming through his centers, and all attraction toward the pleasures of this world vanishes.

Śāktavedha. The So-called Energy Piercing

> 246–247. O Beautiful One! Through *uccāra*[15] of the lower muscles of the trunk [the master] exerts an upward thrust upon the essence of the energy up to the possessor of the energy [Śiva]; then, spontaneously, without any effort of utterance, he lifts the coiled serpentine energy dwelling in the triangular seat. Let him, by her help, pervade the entire universe. Such is the description of the piercing by means of the energy, in which the penetration [resembles] that of the bumble bee.

Without the help of the commentary, this stanza would be incomprehensible; the term *uccāra,* already difficult to translate, here assumes numerous connotations. First, that of an upward contraction by means of the muscles of the rectum (*mattagandha*), with the purpose of making Kuṇḍalinī ascend. *Uccāra* also means a conscious, powerful rising; finally, "*uccāra*-without-*uccāra*" refers to the spontaneous rising of the sound vibration, which occurs without any exertion of the will, which does not require any practice or effort; the energy moves up spontaneously, humming like a bee—both in vibration and in sound.

This piercing, meant for a disciple who wishes to develop his power, is characterized as complete because it goes from lower to higher center while awakening all the wheels. Through a process of contraction and dilatation exerted on the rectum, the *guru* powerfully draws the breath up inside the median way in order to take on the whole energy by seizing the "two feet of Śiva" having a unique savor, in other words, of Śiva in full possession of his energy. In the course of this piercing, the master enters the disciple's body and, while taking his own Kuṇḍalinī upward, he awakens and raises that of the disciple; the latter then feels permeated by a flood of energy of such intensity that it rushes straight along the median way from center to center and, reaching the top of the head, it joins

15. Cf. V.B. *śl.* 24, here p. 39 n.4 *Uccār* –, to rise, to emit, to utter; *uccāra,* release, subtle rising of the breath and the energy, accompanied by sound vibration.

with Śiva, the master of the energy, as perfect consciousness and divine potency have now become inseparable. This is how the *uccāra* of Śiva is achieved.

The distinctive feature of this piercing is its spontaneity, for its attendant sound is like the continuous and natural humming of the black bee. The energy awakens simultaneously in master and disciple, so they have only to focus on this humming sound arising within as the wheels begin to spin and vibrate.

When the ascent is completed, the universe, hitherto latent in a subtle form within the triangle of the lower center (*śṛṅgaṭaka*), now bathes in the universal energy, making it impossible to detect the slightest difference between the divine energy and the universe, so perfect is their commingling.

The next piercing, where Kuṇḍalinī rushes up at once straight to the summit, is also a spontaneous one; for as soon as bliss manifests, all process of penetration necessarily comes to an end, since bliss and spontaneity go hand in hand.

Bhujaṅgavedha. The So-called Serpent Piercing

248–251. This supreme energy blossoming into bliss is adorned like a five-hooded cobra as she rises from the inferior to the superior center. Thus her fivefold aspects are witnessed in functions, in the levels of reality, in lunar days, in centers, in energies (*kula*), in creative causes, in gods [from Brahmā to Sadāśiva], and in organs.

When this energy endowed with five modalties draws herself up from the *brahman*'s [lower] seat and enters the *brahman*'s [higher] seat, she flashes forth like lightning in the former and then dissolves into the latter. Having thus penetrated, let her pierce the body, let her discover the Self. Such is the so-called serpent piercing, as described in the *Bhairavāgama*.

This piercing, although related to the previous one, yields a higher type of awakening—immediate and universal in nature. An overflowing bliss replaces the mystic resonance (*nāda*). The ascending movement, starting from *mūlādhāra* and ending its course in the supreme *dvādaśānta*, does not stop along the intermediate centers; and using the same term "*brahman*" to refer to both the starting and the finishing points only stresses the fact that, during this flashing ascent, the two centers are but one.

The raised energy looks like a cobra whose five hoods, spread out and intensely vibrant, symbolize the numerous facets of the universe: the five *kalā* or spheres of cosmic energies (*śāntātīta, śānta, vidyā, pratiṣṭhā,* and *nivṛtti*),[16] the five *tattva,* from the earth onward, the five *nanda,* or lunar days (*tiṭhi*), the five *vyoman,* namely, *janma,* heart, *bhrū,* and so forth, the five *kula* [the aspects of energy], the five gods of creation [from Brahmā to Sadāśiva], and the organs of cognition and action.

The yogin is endowed with an energy operative in this world (*kriyāśakti*), and his bliss, first permeating his body, now pervades the universe, a universe made of consciousness and one with the Self.

Paravedha. Supreme Piercing

> 252–253. "As long as thought is still resorted to, and until it disappears [the penetration is that of the serpent]; but once it has completely vanished, O Sovereign of the gods! then bliss is called supreme." Henceforth no sense organ, no breath, no inner organ, no thought, no knower and known, and no mental activity. The disappearance of all the modalities of Consciousness, that is regarded as the supreme piercing.

As long as there is penetration, as long as the universe is apprehended by the consciousness endowed with *vikalpa* in the five ways described above, one does not go beyond the so-called serpent initiation. The ultimate stage is the fruit of the previous ones. When the highest piercing takes place, in the absence of

16. Cf. André Padoux, *Recherches sur la Symbolique et l'Energie de la Parole dans certains textes tantriques,* p. 280–82.

mental dichotomy (*vikalpa*), how could a penetration be perceived? If there were one, it would take place everywhere and not in a specific center. When he has reached the one and only Center, the yogin is omnipresent and as his median way is universal, the centers are everywhere and contain everything.

The yogin is no longer aware of his body as being separate from the universe; he does not know where he is; and his *vikalpa* having vanished, he experiences only bliss and indescribable rapture (*nirvikalpacamatkāra*).

Outer Initiations[17]

In his *Tantrāloka,* Abhinavagupta mentions other initiations through piercing. Although of an outer type when compared to those previously described, they do make use of the Kuṇḍalinī energy. Here again, only masters initiated into the mystical secrets (*rahasya*) are qualified to perform them (255).

First there is a piercing by means of mantra (*mantravedha*); the *guru* visualizes the disciple as sitting within a triangular-shaped *maṇḍala,*[18] and by means of the fire phoneme and the seed of illusion, he pierces, with the help of this blazing fire, the knots of the disciple; he then unites him with the supreme Reality (256).

In the next piercing, *śāktavedha,* the *guru* uses the energy to enter into the disciple through one of the three conduits (*nāḍī*), and focuses the whole consciousness in the bulb. Then, moving around and with great impetus, he uses the five organs of action, the eight organs of cognition, and the tuft of hair in order to unite the selected center with this consciousness, now at the summit of the trident of energy (257–258).

In the piercing by means of the form (*rūpavedha*), the master visualizes some image of a divinity shining brightly between the eyebrows, in the *bindu* center; then he must at once identify the disciple with this image. As soon as the disciple clearly perceives this image, he communes with the divinity it represents and ultimately becomes one with it (261–262).

During the piercing through supreme knowledge (*vijñāna-*

17. These initiations are nine in number; however only a few of them are of any relevance here.

18. With the subtle, all-pervading and equal energies as its three corners. Cf. here p. 49.

vedha), because master and disciple are convinced of their identity, the master transfers the eightfold knowledge to the disciple through the subtle thread of his conduits (*nāḍī*), making the sun of a divine knowledge instantly surge forth in the ether of his heart (263–264).

When performing the piercing on certain points of the body (*sthānavedha*), the master rests in each of his disciple's wheels and gradually ignites them, starting from the root center (267).

While there are three chief conduits—*suṣumnā, iḍā,* and *piṅgalā*—those to which they are connected are countless. Piercing by means of the conduits (*nāḍīvedha*) allows the adept to unite with them all. And that is the goal.

The current running through the selected conduit passes through the chief conduits located in the sense organs. This piercing by means of the *nāḍī* produces different forms of awakening (268–269).

Like an animal with a powerful tail, a great yogin, by exploding someone else's conduit curled up in his own conduit, can make even a *siddha*—an accomplished being endowed with supernatural powers—fall to the ground (270).

With the supreme piercing (*paravedha*), the *guru,* bestower of divine nature, reveals the supreme Śiva to one who, in a state free of all duality, becomes intensely aware of the highest piercing involving all the centers (271).

Abhiṣeka, Consecration

We have yet to deal with the highest form of initiation, where the master works on the disciple's energy after bestowing upon him the grace by which he becomes a master (*ācārya*) fit to initiate many disciples in his turn.

The purpose of the ceremony described by Abhinavagupta[19] is the identification of the disciple with the master "just as a torch is kindled by another torch," the disciple emulating his master in every possible way: mystical experiences, knowledge, behavior, character traits, and so forth.

After the anointing, the *guru* infuses into this new master the power of the mantra (*mantravīrya*). To prepare for this, the latter must spend six months meditating on all the formulas; and by

19. T. A. Ch. XXIII, śl. 1–39, a condensed version of which is given here.

identifying with the mantra, he shares its power which is essential to break his bonds. Then he returns to his master and sits in front of him; at this point a heart-to-heart initiation takes place, not unlike the piercing through resonance (*nādavedha*) previously described.[20]

> 33–40. From the heart wheel of the *guru*, the vital energy rises up like a straight line, being the essence of sound, subtle and akin to a moon-crystal [that is, to a beneficial nectar, clear and pure]. Appeased, it passes through the successive centers, and inside the median way rushes up to the superior center. [There, within the very breath energy, the master fills the disciple's heart with this mantric essence].
>
> Then he emits the mantra, which shines like a vivid flame and springs forth from all the apertures of the body . . . At last satisfied, the point of the flame subdues in the Heart[21] center once the butter it fed upon has completely melted away.

So, through the *uccāra* of the breath energy, the *guru* instills the sound essence of the new *ācārya* into his chief centers, from the root center to *tālu,* following the main stages of the *Oṃ* energy[22]—the last of which gives him access to the supreme Śiva. Whatever center is worked upon by the master, the mantra proves efficient. When infused into the *sādhaka,* this mantra comes back to the master's heart, and from there moves up to his *brahmarandhra,* down again to his heart, and then returns to the disciple's heart, in a continuous back and forth movement between *guru* and initiate.

Through this consecration related to the pure Science (*vidyā*), the new master acquires the power of the mystical formulas, so that any mantra he will give to his own disciples will itself prove to be potent, pure, and capable of setting them free.

20. Cf. here p. 94.

21. Textually, "navel", glossed as "Heart."

22. Namely *ardhendu, rodhikā, nāda, nādānta, śakti, vyāpinī, samanā* and *unmanā*.

Vedhadīkṣā

Vedhadīkṣā ca bahudhā tatra tatra nirūpitā ı
sā cābhyāsavatā kāryā yenordhvordvapraveśataḥ ıı *237*

śiṣyasya cakrasaṃbhedapratyayo jāyate dhruvaḥ ı
yenāṇimādikā siddhiḥ śrīmālāyāṃ ca coditā ıı *238*

ūrdhvacakradaśālābhe piśācāveśa eva sā ı
mantranādabinduśaktibhujaṅgamaparātmikā ıı *239*

ṣoḍhā śrīgahvare vedhadīkṣoktā parameśinā ı
jvālākulaṃ svaśāstroktaṃ cakram aṣṭārakādikam ıı *240*

Dhyātvā tenāsya hṛccakravedhanān mantravedhanam ı
ākāraṃ navadhā dehe nyasya saṃkramayet tataḥ ıı *241*

nyāsayogena śiṣyāya dīpyamānaṃ mahārciṣam ı
pāśas tobhāt tatas tasya paratattve tu yojanam ıı *242*

iti dīkṣottare dṛṣṭo vidhir me śaṃbhunoditaḥ ı
nādoccāreṇa nādākhyaḥ sṛṣṭikramaniyogataḥ ıı *243*

nādena vedhayec cittaṃ nādavedha udīritaḥ ı
bindusthānagataṃ cittaṃ bhrūmadhyapathasaṃsthitam ıı *244*

hṛllakṣye vā maheśāni binduṃ jvālākulaprabham ı
tena sambodhayet sādhyaṃ bindvākhyo 'yaṃ prakīrtitaḥ ıı *245*

śāktaṃ śaktimaduccārād gandhoccāreṇa sundari ı
śṛṅgāṭakāsanasthaṃ tu kuṭilaṃ kuṇḍalākṛtim ıı *246*

anuccāreṇa coccārya vedhayen nikhilaṃ jagat ı
evaṃ bhramaravedhena śāktavedha udāhṛtaḥ ıı *247*

sā caiva paramā śaktir ānandapravikāsinī ı
janmasthānāt paraṃ yāti phaṇapañcakabhūṣitā ıı *248*

kalās tattvāni nandādyā vyomāni ca kulāni ca |
brahmādikāraṇāny akṣāṇy eva sā pañcakātmikā || *249*

evaṃ pañcaprakārā sā brahmasthānavinirgatā |
brahmasthāne viśāntī tu taḍillīnā virājate || *250*

praviṣṭhā vedhayet kāyam ātmānaṃ pratibhedayet |
evaṃ bhujaṅgavedhas tu kathito bhairavāgame || *251*

tāvad bhāvayate cittaṃ yāvac cittaṃ kṣayaṃ gatam |
kṣīṇe citte sureśāni parānanda udāhṛtaḥ || *252*

nendriyāṇi na vai prāṇāntaḥkaraṇagocaraḥ |
na mano nāpi mantavyaṃ na mantā na manikriyā || *253*

sarvabhāvaparikṣīṇaḥ paravedha udāhṛtaḥ ||

Chapter Two

Somānanda's *Śāktavijñāna*

Discriminative knowledge related to the energy[1]

[The thirteen movements or stages of Kuṇḍalinī are as follows:]

> 1–2. Seat, penetration, aspect, object [of contemplation], symptoms, the act of raising [Kuṇḍalinī], awakening, rest in the centers, access to the stages, final state [of the energy], rest, radical change, and finally origin or return.
>
> 3. The highest discriminative knowledge related to the [Kuṇḍalinī] energy thus comprises thirteen stages. And in all the Trika scriptures they are referred to by Śiva himself.

1. Edited from a *sharada* manuscript together with the *Parātrīśikātātparyadīpikā* of unknown authorship, in the Kashmir Series of Texts and Studies, pp. 47–49, by Pandit Jagaddhar Zadoo, 1947, Śrinagar.

I

Sthāna. Seat or Station

4. Five fingers' breadth below the navel and two above the sexual organ, there between these two, is situated the bulb known as *cakrasthāna,* the seat of the lower center.

II

Praveśa. Penetration [of Kuṇḍalinī]

5. After the inspired and expired breaths have been stilled, let the thought be focused on this very spot.[2] When the movement of the breath is completely under control, to the point of it being guided into the median way, this is what is called "penetration."

III

Rūpa. Aspect

6. Now I am going to describe the aspect thereof. [It consists of two centers]: one looks like the triangular water chestnut,[3] and the other, permanent, possesses six spokes.

7. The bulb (*kanda*) looks like the flower of a pomegranate; it is red in type and [pure] contemplation in essence. In the enumeration, its aspect is the third [stage].

2. The previous station.

3. Within the bulb both sexes reside: that of the adept, looking like the *śṛṅgaṭaka*—the fruit of the water-chestnut, symbolic of the triangle (*trikoṇa*)—and that of the opposite sex, symbolized by a six-spoked figure, the seal of Solomon; thus it contains one's own sex and the complementary sex. About the *ṣaṭkoṇa,* cf. here pp. 33, 199.

IV

Lakṣa. Object [of Contemplation]

8. Let the thought be focused in the middle of this bulb, until it is firmly grounded there, and as the breath, having been first relinquished,[4] becomes still, the [pursued] goal stands revealed.

V

Lakṣaṇa. Symptom or Characteristic Sign

9. The energy made of unstruck sound (*anāhata*) stands in the middle, in the wheel of the bulb, looking like a straight line with serpentine undulations at both ends, above and below.

10. [This] state [of immobility] thus settles below and above. Between those two [that are sun and moon], the *kalā*[5] is indeed resplendent with a brilliance equal to that of a thousand suns.

11. This energy can be ascertained by slightly restraining the breath [inside]. That is what is referred to as "symptom."

And now the supreme ascent:

VI

Utthāpana. The Act of Raising

12. And, while engaged in the practice of expiring [the inward breath], let one repeat the for-

4. *Tyakta*, forsaken, cast aside.

5. *Kalā* is the divine energy, in the sense of a lunar portion, the sixteenth, that shines brightly Cf. *Hymnes aux Kālī*, pp. 41–42 and 188.

mula [*Oṃ, akṣa, hrīṃ*] and concentrate upon the fully awakened energy, the supreme Goddess, [straight] like a staff.

13. Arising from the middle of the [root] support, she rests in the *suṣumnā* channel. This is what is referred to as "*utthāpana,*" the act of raising. And now the Awakening:

VII

Bodhana. Awakening

14. Now when she is in the bulb, she must successively pierce her way through the navel, then through Brahmā situated in the heart, then through Viṣṇu, the unshakable, standing in the throat, and with no delay let her enter Rudra seated at the vault of the palate

15. Then let her enter Īśvara, standing between the eyebrows, and penetrate into Sadāśiva through the gate of *brahman*. Once awakened, let her quickly reach the realm of the unrelated Śiva.

VIII

Cakraviśramaṇa. Repose in the Centers

16. That is what is called awakening. Now, repose in the [various] centers. The energy pierces the *brahmarandhra,* [lotus with a thousand] petals,[6] dazzling, innate, fluid and [yet] similar to the immutable firmament.

17. This is the immortal diadem[7] and also

6. *Dala,* "lotus shoot," that which unfolds spontaneously, but also (lotus) "petal," referring to the thousand-petalled lotus in the *sahasrāra*.

7. The crown of the head.

the energy, besides being *brahman* itself; this is *bindu* and *nāda* [Śiva and the energy]. Such indeed is what is known as the twelve wheels.

18. When the energy has pierced the wheels in succession, let this great Goddess take her rest in each for a while.

With relation to the wheels, this is the best repose.

IX
Bhūmikāgamana. Access to the Stages

19. At first the heart trembles: next the gate of the palate itself, together with the head, starts to spin. Then in this [yogin][8] appears the symptom of having transcended ordinary vision.

20. He lets each part of his body oscillate, his limbs at the joints too and his heart flutters under the supernatural influence of the integral Science.

21. Whatever the modifications produced by such a state, let one not be afraid of them; this is the Sovereign's play.

22. Intoxicated by the ambrosia, she brings about those numerous modifications resulting from actions performed through many births, according to the modification of the three energies.

23. [The yogin] shakes the bonds related to the impurity stirred up by the supreme energy. Such is what is known as the access to the stages. Now the final state will be explained:

X
Antāvasthā. Final State

24. When he reaches this final stage, various

8. Instead of *satas* (of this being), should we read *yatas*?

manifestations arise unexpectedly from the bulb: horripilation, floods of tears, tendency to yawn, stammering, bursting of the knots, divine joy of touch, and vibrations in the *bindu.*[9]

XI

Viśrama. Perfect Repose

25–26. The final state has just been explained; now comes the description of repose: when the energy arising from the navel center fully awakes, at once[10] all the outward-directed organs are gone, while the supreme energy dissolves in the supreme abode.

27. When the subject no longer discovers any other object to be known [apart from himself] and when his energy rests in Śiva, that is called "repose."

XII

Pariṇāma. Radical Change

28. If, at the very place where the energy found repose, absorption of thought is achieved, then for those beings endowed with certitude, it is in its nature of absolute Self that the Self must be known.

29. When the Self is *parama* Śiva himself, that is precisely what is meant by radical change, for it is he who continuously pours the celestial ambrosia, the Life of human beings.

9. That is to say *vīrya.* Cf. my commentary.
10. Read *tadāśu.*

XIII

Āgamana. Return

30. But consciousness should be held at this place for this divine energy will penetrate there again. Such is her final return.

Thus has been given the whole teaching about the thirteen [stages].

Such is the full text of *Discriminative Knowledge Related to the [Kuṇḍalinī] Energy* by the venerable Somānanda.

May writers and readers be prosperous!

Analysis of the *Śaktavijñāna*

The *Śaktavijñāna*, without mentioning the breath accumulation in *tālu*, begins its description of Kuṇḍalinī's ascent with the penetration of the breath right into the root center or the median way.

I-II. To raise Kuṇḍalinī one should engage in continuous contemplation (*cintanā*), for in her essence she is contemplation. Then one visualizes the so-called "birth" triangle (*janmādhāra*), whose naturally downward-turned apex must be reversed just as the breath enters it and Kuṇḍalinī stretches up. If this triangle is not used for concentration, it will gradually fade away; but if attention is fixed upon it while the raising of Kuṇḍalinī is attempted, it becomes solid, firm, and steady. Subsequently it changes into a six-spoked wheel (*ṣaḍāra*), when the energy and Śiva become inseparably united.

III. *Rūpa*, aspect: This center is red because red is indicative of the awakening of Kuṇḍalinī. The first stages take place in *mūlādhāra*.

IV. *Lakṣa*, the object of contemplation, is the still-unformulated goal toward which one is groping; it begins to discover itself when the one-pointed thought is firmly fixed on the bulb and when the breath subsides of its own accord. It becomes still even without the least effort to be aware of it.

Such is the meaning of *tyakta,* forsaken, cast aside in a natural way; one simply forgets to breathe. Indeed, if the breath is stopped willfully before it has first been appeased, life will be endangered.

V. *Lakṣaṇa,* symptom: At the stage of penetration, the *prāṇa* or vital force shoots forth to the root center. Henceforth it remains there, still, with no trace of inspiration or expiration, and Kuṇḍalinī, thus, lies motionless. Only a sound vibration moves through the coiled one, from head to tail, the spontaneous *anāhata* sound springing up from within.

Kuṇḍalinī is serpentine, coiled-up[11] in the manner of a snake. She has two extremities, which seems to mean that the yogin, from head to foot, experiences nothing but Kuṇḍalinī as she lies motionless between the two poles of sun and moon, encompassing *prāṇa, apāna,* and all duality.

Thus appeased, Kuṇḍalinī assumes a most wonderful brilliance.[12] The symptom of this state is the quiescence of the energy; this perfect quiescence can be easily ascertained by a slight breath retention,[13] *manāk,* "somewhat," that is, by keeping the air in the lungs naturally and smoothly, without exerting any external pressure or any effort whatsoever. And the same goes for the next stage:

VI. *Utthāpana,* the act of raising. Kuṇḍalinī draws herself up to the entrance to the median way through spiritual energy alone and not by means of breath exercises. A deep absorption (*samādhi*) very naturally induces the straightening which cannot occur but in the median way.

Expiration of the inner breath (*antaḥrecaka*)—the void at the end of expiration—infuses the necessary power for Kuṇḍalinī to become as rigid as a staff. To this end, the yogin recites the formula *Oṃ, akṣa, hriṃ. Oṃ* is the well-known *praṇava, akṣa* contains all the phonemes from *A* to *KṢ,* and is therefore the *mātṛkā,* the Life of the phonemes, while *hriṃ* is the Kuṇḍalinī mantra.

At the same time, the yogin beholds both extremities of the coiled one and concentrates on the act of raising seeing her uncoil and stretch up.

Kuṇḍalinī, it should be noted, moves no further up than the root center and rests in the median channel. That is the stage of bliss.

11. *Kuṭilā.*
12. Cf. V.B. śl 37.
13. *Kumbhaka.*

VII. Then, at the stage of awakening (*bodhana*), the energy rises from the bulb to the superior center.

The *Svacchandatantra*[14] describes the same stages as well as the divinities or energies of the Lord which preside over them: Brahmā in the heart, Viṣṇu in the throat, Rudra in the palate, Īśvara in the center between the eyebrows, and the eternal Śiva (Sadāśiva) in the *brahmarandhra*. In addition to this, the *Śaktavijñāna* mentions the unrelated Śiva (*anāśritaśiva*) situated in the Void beyond all void.[15]

Those divinities preside over specific functions within the body.

VIII. Next comes repose in the superior center, an innate, resplendent petal—now undulating, now immobile, and also both at the same time since it is the All.

Here the twelve wheels are those six related to the subtle body, *mūlādhāra*, and so forth; as for the six cosmic wheels that rise from earth up to Sadāśiva, they are located at points that correspond to those of the subtle body.

Having described the centers, the author now turns to the various movements of Kuṇḍalinī and the manifestations produced during her ascent from wheel to wheel, which she quickens as she passes through them.

IX. When access to the stages of yoga is gained, the powerful energy pierces and penetrates[16] each wheel, for as long as it does not permeate the 72,000 subtle channels, the yogin is subject to strange alterations, as the center is first touched, then opened, and finally fully awakened.

If while freely moving up it stops for a few minutes at each wheel and causes it to vibrate, during the long period of preparation, and when a center is pierced for the first time, certain, often spectacular, disturbances do occur; under the terrific pressure of the ascending Kuṇḍalinī and the extreme tension she generates, the body can react in unpredictable ways. Thus a violent tremor spreads from the heart; then the vault of the palate starts vibrating. And just as the yogin becomes omnipresent, he feels dizzy[17]—a stage indicating celestial sight (*divyadṛṣṭi*), which pierces through everything unobstructed. And again, under the influence of the pure

14. IV- Ś1 258 seq. Cf. T.A. VI. 187.
15. *Śūnyātiśūnya*.
16. According to the double meaning of *vyādh*–.
17. Cf. here p. 74.

mystic Science, the limbs oscillate at the joints,[18] the heart throbs when the yogin shifts from the individual to the universal state.[19]

All of these transformations affecting the yogin are not to be feared; this is but Kuṇḍalinī who, totally intoxicated by the nectar of bliss, playfully assumes those varied forms. Having lost her composure, she knocks forcefully at the doors of the centers, and finding her way obstructed, arouses unexpected effects. The obstacles on the path are the knots due to impurities accumulated from a distant past. Consequently the reaction of each individual is dependent in part upon the latent tendencies from past lives. After having shaken the bonds until they break altogether, Kuṇḍalinī finds access to the final stage:

X. Final state. From certain symptoms it may be inferred that the energy is rising: a flood of tears, horripilation, spontaneous half-opening of the mouth as at the time of death. Also it may happen that, while engaged in conversation, the yogin begins to stammer, to utter inarticulate words, to speak in a voice broken with sobs of joy.

The knots burst open in those centers that no longer resist the penetration. How divine the sensation when Kuṇḍalinī, permeating the 72,000 *nāḍī,* pours bliss into the entire body. Finally sparks full of power (*vīrya*) spout from the bulb; this scintillation occurs when vibrations (*spanda*) course through the centers. *Binduvīrya* also alludes to the inner practice of virile potency that rises through the median way to the *brahmarandhra.*

XI. At the stage of rest (*viśrāma*), when Kuṇḍalinī, leaving the navel center, fully awakens, all the sense organs, no longer turned outward, merge into the pure subjective energy, much like the sun setting on the horizon. Once the energy subsides, all the organs naturally calm down, outwardly-turned activity and dichotomized thought no longer exist.

Upon reaching the supreme *dvādaśānta* the energy is absorbed into Śiva, while secondary wheels and centers merge and flow as a single unit inside the median way. At this stage of oneness, or pure consciousness (*cit*), the yogin experiences a peace henceforth indestructible.

XII. The stage next to last consists of a radical change (*pari-*

18. Also mentioned by Saint John of the Cross.

19. One feels as if a bird is flitting inside one's chest, but there are no actual heart palpitations. Cf. here p. 58, where *ghūrṇi* is related to the divine and omnipresent Heart.

ṇāma), when thought (*manas*), absorbed in this state of rest, disappears, and the yogin makes his final shift from the limited to the unlimited, from the discovery of the Self (*ātman*) to that of the absolute Self (*paramātman*), realizing with full awareness his identity with Paramaśiva, the universal Self. The Self then continuously pours the celestial ambrosia.

What is the difference, then, between verse 28 and *śloka* 29-30? The former deals with a state related to practice (*sādhanāvasthā*), whereas the latter refers to an easy and spontaneous realization (*siddhāvasthā*).

XIII. *Āgamana*. The double meaning of the root of this term, *āgam-*, return and origin, conveys accordingly the idea of an oncoming, which is but the return to the origin. If thought is concentrated on this cosmic state, the divine energy once again pervades with full spontaneity all worldly activities (*jantujīvana* of verse 29), being their very Life. Thus, from a limited starting point one gains access to the unlimited and, endowed with a divinized Consciousness, comes back to the starting point, henceforth apprehended as unlimited.

शाक्तविज्ञानं

श्रीसोमानन्दनाथविरचितम् ।

स्थानं प्रवेशो रूपं च लक्ष्यं लक्षणमेव च ।
उत्थापनं बोधनं च चक्रविश्राममेव च ॥ १ ॥
भूमिकागमनं चैव अन्तावस्था तथैव च ।
विश्रामः परिणामश्च तथागमनमेव च ॥ २ ॥
इति त्रयोदशविधं शाक्तं विज्ञानमुत्तमम् ।
सर्वेषु त्रिकशास्त्रेषु सूचितं शम्भुना स्वयम् ॥ ३ ॥
नाभ्यध अङ्गुलाः पञ्च मेढ्रस्योर्ध्वाङ्गुलद्वयम् ।
तन्मध्ये कन्दनामा च चक्रस्थानमिति स्मृतम् ॥ ४ ॥
प्राणापाननिरोधेन मनस्तत्रैव निःक्षिपेत् ।
सम्यग् वायुगतिं जित्वा यावन्मध्यगतां नयेत् ॥ ५ ॥
एष प्रवेश इत्याहु रूपं वक्ष्यामि चाधुना ।
शृङ्गाटकनिभं चक्रं षडरं चापरं ध्रुवम् ॥ ६ ॥
दाडिमीकुसुमप्रख्यं कन्दं वै जातिलोहितम् ।
एतद्रूपं समाख्यातं तृतीयं चिन्तनात्मकम् ॥ ७ ॥
तन्मध्ये निक्षिपेच्चित्तं यावत्तत्र स्थिरीकृतम् ।
त्यक्तरुद्धो यदा वायुस्तदा लक्ष्यं विनिर्दिशेत् ॥ ८ ॥
कन्दचक्रस्य मध्यस्था स्वनाहतमयी कला ।
अधोर्ध्वे रेखासंयुक्ता भुजङ्गकुटिलाकृतिः ॥ ९ ॥
ऊर्ध्वाधोऽवस्थितावस्था सूर्याचन्द्रमसावुभौ ।
सत्यं विराजमाना सा सहस्रार्कसमप्रभा ॥ १० ॥

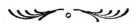

तामेवालोकयेच्छक्तिं मनाक् कुम्भकवृत्तिना ।
एतल्लक्षणमुद्दिष्टमुत्थापनमतः परम् ॥ ११ ॥
जुषद्रेचकवृत्त्या तु मन्त्रं चैव समुच्चरेत् ।
प्रबुद्धां चिन्तयेच्छक्तिं दण्डवत्परमेश्वरीम् ॥ १२ ॥
आधारमध्यादायाता सुषुम्नामार्गमाश्रिता ।
उत्थापनं समाख्यातं बोधनं परतस्तथा ॥ १३ ॥
कन्दस्थां वेधयेन्नाभिं ततो हृत्स्थं पितामहम् ।
कण्ठस्थमच्युतं साक्षाद्रुद्रं तालुतले स्थितम् ॥ १४ ॥
भ्रुवोर्मध्यगतं स्वीशं ब्रह्मद्वारे सदाशिवम् ।
बोधयित्वा व्रजेदाशु पदं चानाश्रितं शिवम् ॥ १५ ।
एतद्बोधनमुद्दिष्टं चक्रविश्रामणं ततः ।
स्वाभाविकं दलं दीप्तं द्रवं स्थिरनभोपमम् ॥ १६ ॥
अमृतं शेखरं चैव शक्तिर्ब्रह्मा तथैव च ।
बिन्दुनादं तथा प्रोक्तं चक्रद्वादशकं किल ॥ १७ ॥
वेधयन्ती क्रमाच्छक्तिश्चक्रे चक्रे प्रतिक्षणम् ।
विश्रमेत्सा महादेवी चक्रविश्राम उत्तमः ॥ १८ ॥
हृदयं कम्पते पूर्वं तालुकद्वारमेव च ।
शिरश्च भ्रमते तस्य दृष्टिसंक्रान्तिलक्षणम् ॥ १९ ॥
एकैकं भ्रमयत्यङ्गमङ्गप्रत्यङ्गसन्धिषु ।
घूर्णते हृदयं चास्य सम्यग्विद्याप्रभावतः ॥ २० ॥
यानि यानि विकाराणि अवस्था कुरुते सतः ।
तेषु तेषु म भेतव्यं क्रीडति परमेश्वरी ॥ २१ ॥
अमृते सेयमुन्मत्ता विकारान् कुरुते बहून् ।
मलत्रयविकारेण बहुजन्मसु यत्कृतम् ॥ २२ ॥

धुनोति समलान् पाशात् परशक्तिसमुत्थितान् ।
भूमिकागमनं प्रोक्तमन्तावस्था तथोच्यते ॥ २३ ॥

यत्संक्रान्तौ रोमहर्षोऽस्रुपातो
जृम्भारम्भो गद्गदा गीर्गिरोऽन्तः ।
ग्रन्थिस्फोटः स्पर्शादिव्यप्रहर्षौ
बिन्दुस्पन्दा नाभिकन्दात् स्फुरन्ति ॥ २४ ॥

अन्तावस्था समाख्याता विश्रामस्त्वधुनोच्यते ।
नाभिचक्रविनिर्याता यदा शक्तिः प्रबुध्यते ॥ २५ ॥
तदा त्वस्तमितं सर्वमक्षग्रामं बहिः स्थितम् ।
यदा सा परमा शक्तिः सुलीना परमे पदे ॥ २६ ॥
तदा न विन्दते किञ्चिद्विषयी विषयान्तरम् ।
शिवे विश्राम्यते शक्तिस्तदा विश्राम उच्यते ॥ २७ ॥
यत्र विश्रमणं शक्तेर्मनस्तत्र लयं व्रजेत् ।
तदात्मा परमात्मत्वे ज्ञातव्यो निश्चितात्मभिः ॥ २८ ॥
शिवीभूतो भवत्यात्मा परिणामः स एवहि ।
सदा स वर्षते दिव्यममृतं जन्तुजीवनम् ॥ २९ ॥
चित्तं तत्र तु सन्धार्य पुनर्देवी विशेत्तु सा ।
तदा त्वागमनं प्रोक्तमेवं सम्यक् त्रयोदश ॥ ३० ॥

इति श्रीसोमानन्दपादविरचितं
शाक्तविज्ञानं संपूर्णम् ॥
शिवमस्तु लेखकपाठकयोः ॥

Chapter Three

Gorakṣanātha's *Amaraughaśāsana*

The Nātha

What follows is but a brief account of the origins of the Kula school—that of the Nātha—and its founder, Matsyendranātha or Macchandanātha, who revealed the sacred texts belonging to this mystical school.[1]

Abhinavagupta's *Tantrāloka* opens with a tribute to this great "fisherman" who destroyed the net of illusion:

"May Macchandanātha be propitious to me," says he, "he who tore apart the glowing net made of knots and holes, a batch of bits and pieces unfolding and spreading everywhere" (I.7).

Matsyendra revived the Yoginīkaula sect and preached his doctrine in Assam. Is he the author of the *Kaulajñānanirṇaya,* the *caryā* and the *dohā* of the Sahajīya cult? Is he that Minanātha who wrote the *Yogaviṣaya?* His date cannot be ascertained; he may have lived between the eighth and tenth centuries.

His disciple, Gorakṣanātha,[2] was held in great reverence in North India as an accomplished being (*siddha*). He wrote the *Siddhasiddhāntapaddhati,* the *Amaraughaprabodha* ("Awakening Re-

1. For further details, cf. *Corps subtil et corps causal,* Tara Michaël, Le Courrier du Livre, Paris, p. 41 ff.

2. Abhinavagupta does not mention his name in his list of *siddha.* Does this mean that Abhinavagupta precedes Gorakṣa's time?

vealing Immortality"). We have no hesitation in also ascribing to him the *Amaraughaśāsana,* "Immortal Flow," which keeps death away and enables one to conquer time. It enables the yogin to become aware of nonduality and quickly reach the efficience precisely called *amaraughasiddhi.*

Since they apply the name *śivagotra* to themselves, the Nātha are Śaivites. To them Śiva, as pure Consciousness, enjoys quietude and eternity, whereas Śakti, his energy, is the source of change and of the varied experiences related to it.

The Nātha have as their goal liberation in life. The steps taken toward this end are simple. They advocate neither outer religious practices nor scriptural knowledge. Their only emphasis is on a direct path, as short as possible, a way which the mystic discovers within himself, right in his own body—the privileged place for experience, whether of the Godhead, the energy, or the universe.

To this end the Nātha resort to but one means: intuition and *sahajasamādhi,* the spontaneous absorption. Therefore they are called "*Sahajīya*," adepts of spontaneity. Simplicity of heart and mind is their distinctive feature. Through *sahajasamādhi* thought becomes absorbed in bliss, the false sense of objectivity and duality weakens and ultimately disappears.

When this type of *samādhi* prevails in all daily activities, the yogin, whatever the circumstances, experiences one and the same savor (*samarasa*) permeating the entire universe.

This is why it is necessary to sanctify, to transfigure the body, for to acquire supernatural powers the body must be pure, refined, and adamantine. But here again, there is no need of arduous *haṭhayoga* practices. Breath control is achieved through the *kumbhakamudrā,* by infusing the breaths into the *suṣumnā* channel through the unifying friction of the ascendant and descendant breaths, which no longer function within duality: this is an effortless practice; when thought becomes still, so do the senses. As for sex control, it is achieved through inner repetition (*ajapājapa*); indeed, once everything has merged into the median way, the yogin perceives an inner spontaneous sound (*anāhatanāda*), and if he keeps on listening to it, Kuṇḍalinī awakens and rushes to the superior center where she unites with Śiva.

In this way he attains easily, naturally, innately (*sahaja*) the *unmanī* energy which is beyond thought, and he becomes a liberated being, an *avadhūta* ("unattached").

But to obtain this state a *guru* belonging to the *siddha* lineage is absolutely necessary: he must be revered as equal to Śiva himself. He is the one who, without any exertion on his part, achieves in his disciple holding of the breath, absorption of the mind and the awakening of Kuṇḍalinī.

Since such practices must be kept secret, the Nātha use a language known as "intentional," which is merely allusive and so doeṣ not make sense but for a true, initiated disciple. Accordingly, the texts are usually very terse, deliberately cryptic, and abstruse.

The *Amaraughaśāsana* does not follow a definite pattern; the description of the centers is mixed with that of Kuṇḍalinī's motions, while the quotations contribute to the overall obscureness. It is true that, in a way, all that relates to a center should be stated at one time, thus making it difficult to avoid apparent confusion.

Amaraughaśāsana

Excerpts

Summary of the first nine pages:

> It is by assailing the ascending energy and by means of the inferior or descending Kuṇḍalinī, as well as by awakening the median way energy that supreme bliss is generated.

When the ascending and descending breaths (*prāṇa* and *apāna*) are forced toward the heart, the median energy expands in the central way (*suṣumnā*).

Next, Gorakṣa deals with generalities of little relevance here; he enumerates the bodily elements (earth, water, fire, air, and ether) and their fivefold quality; the ten breaths (*vata*), namely: *prāṇa, apāna, samāna, udāna, vyāna,* and at a deeper level those related to the mind and not to the body: *nāga, kūrma, kṛkara, devadatta,* and *dhanañjaya.*[3]

Of the 72,000 *nāḍī* Gorakṣa gives the names of the ten chief ones: *iḍā, piṅgalā, suṣumnā, gāndhārī, hastijihvā, yaśasvinī, pūṣā, ālambusā, kuhū,* and *śaṅkhinī.*[4]

3. According to the *Yogaviṣaya* (13–14), the first five are associated with the five organs of action peculiar to the energy of activity; the other five, at a deeper level, depend upon the five organs of cognition and are related to intellectual energy (*buddhi*). In the *Mārtaṇḍagrantha,* Gorakṣa locates *prāṇa* in the heart, *apāna* in the anus, *samāna* in the navel, *ūdana* in the throat, and *vyāna* in the whole body. *Nāga* might be "that which grasps," *kūrma* manifests in wonder and fear, Abhinavagupta relates it to contraction. *Kṛkara* produces hunger, and *devadatta* yawning. *Dhanañjaya* remains in the corpse until it is burned.

4. About these various *nāḍī,* cf. *Yogamaṇḍala grantha,* p. 85–87, edited with the *Siddhasiddhāntapaddhati* and the *Yogaviṣaya* by Smt Kalyani Mallik, and entitled *Siddha-Siddhānta-Paddhati and Other Works of Nath Yogis.* Poona, Oriental Book House, 1954.

Then comes the enumeration of ties, of essences, of human nature (desire, bliss, discrimination, horripilation, and so on), as well as of humors and other bodily constituents, including hairs, and lastly of ten apertures: nostrils, eyes, ears, throat, mouth, sex, and anus.

> But the tenth, a subtle aperture, is twofold: *kālamārga,*[5] the way of time and the way of *vīrya,* semen, characterized as the way of nectar or bliss.
>
> At the root of the *brahmadaṇḍa* [*brahman's* staff], or *madhyanāḍī* in the center of sun and moon, resides that which has a propitious form (*bhagākāra*).

Next Gorakṣa deals with sexuality: the way of *rajas* for women and the way of *retas* for men. In man and woman alike this way has a threefold aspect: desire, poison, and the unconditioned, which remains undefiled.[6]

At the end of page 9, Gorakṣa comes to the heart of the matter, explaining the various characteristics of *śaṅkhinī*—that is, Kuṇḍalinī—as related to the activity of the root center.

> Between the anus and the sexual organ sits the *trikoṇa* with three circles around it. And there, in that triangle, are perceived one, two, three knots of this root [basis]. In the middle of the three knots sits a lotus with four downward-turned petals. There, in the center of the pericarp, is found a conch of extreme subtlety, like the fiber of a lotus stem, wherein rests the Kuṇḍalinī energy, the coiled one, resembling a very young shoot. The latter, in the form of two or three conduits (*nāḍī*), after entering the seed of consciousness, lies dormant."

5. *Kālamārga* both generates and squeezes time, for it is the cause of breath, which in turn is the origin of time. Does it refer here to the *vyāna* breath, which, as it permeates the entire body, gives it life and flexibility?

6. As for *kāma, viṣa* and *nirañjana* associated with sexual practices, cf. here p. 140, Gorakṣa seems to follow the Tantra on this point.

Verses from Page 10

"There she dwells, in the middle of the triple path [the root of the three conduits], as subtle as a spider's thread: moving up a distance of four fingers' breadth to the navel circle, she folds eight times; then, from the navel center, she sends forth numerous branches, chief and secondary.

In the middle of the navel, there is a wheel resting upon ten conduits, including *iḍā, piṅgalā,* and *suṣumnā.* These ascending branches are supported by a main branch, the *merudaṇḍa.* One of them, the *alambusā,* is also supported by this branch."

So Kuṇḍalinī, made up of innumerable conduits, is carried away into the vortex of the *brahman* or whirling center.

(Text in Prose at the End of Page 10)

"Along the central channel, this path [of Kuṇḍalinī] extends up to the braincase; there, in the moon circle, resides the supreme *liṅga* of the skull. From above the seat of *lampikā* (uvula), this *liṅga* showers nectar. In the inner space, the *garbha* situated in the middle of the forehead, is found that very nectar. Having mastered it on the surface of the *brahmadaṇḍa,* similar to an ivory tusk (*rājadanta*), *śaṅkhinī*[7] releases its flow (p. 11).

Inside the *rājadanta* there is but one orifice, the mouth of *śaṅkhinī,* known as the tenth door.

From the circle of the root portion whence the Kuṇḍalinī energy flows out [in the center of *mūlādhāra*] spring up the moon conduit from the left portion, and the sun conduit from the

7. Conch, namely, Kuṇḍalinī.

right portion. The moon fills up the left portion of the body and the sun the right one. The moon is said to be related to the cavity of the left nostril and the sun to that of the right nostril. This is how moon and sun are established.

From the root bulb arises breath, arises thought, arises the sun, arises life (*jīva*), arise sound and *mātṛkākṣara.*

Within the mind lies the realm of mystic sleep; the function of the indescribable supreme Self is will (*icchā*)."

(Verses from Page 11)

"Ascending from the root bulb, the breath moves up along the path of moon and sun. Supported by the energy, it finds access to the *brahmadaṇḍa (suṣumnā)* and pierces it. This breath that spirals upward is called *prāṇa* by the awakened ones.

By means of the bulb staff, this unconscious coiled one whirls around under the action of the staff-bearers [the breaths]. Thus, impelled by them, she recognizes Śiva."

(Verses from Pages 10 and 11)

"The *liṅga,* situated below the seat of birth, abides in the middle of the root bulb and above the sexual organ. Above, is the seat of the *liṅga,* the *svādhiṣṭhāna,* 'the pleasant one;' in the navel region, in the upper part of the center full of gems (*maṇipūra*), resides the fire. This is why, first of all, this fire, carrying the raised staff, blazes up from all sides.

In the lower region of *maṇipūra,* facing south and north, is the anus[8] area. And in its middle, the navel bulb in the form of a lotus is said to be the receptacle of all bodily currents [the *nāḍi*].

In the heart lotus dwells the earth category, yellow in color, and in the middle, red like a *kadamba* flower, sits the fire wheel, resting place for the empirical consciousness. In the throat, the seat of purification, is located the category of the Self overrun by the wave of [lustral] water.

In the middle the vault of the palate (*tālu*), like the tapering flame of a candle, the category of fiery effulgence (*tejas*) shines continuously.

Within the bud emerging from the cavity of the cranial bulb resides the air category, and at the tip of the nose, that of ether. Above, in *bhrū,* is the seat of command *(ājñā).* In this seat, within sixteen knots,[9] is found the nectar of the sixteenth lunar portion; and within this *kalā* rests the cognitive energy subtler than the hundredth part of the tip of a hair. Above this energy dwells the dot, *bindu* [or virile potency, *vīrya*].

When the *bindu* explodes and shatters, it expands immediately and forms the *mastaka* [that is, the *brahmarandhra*], similar to the triangular fruit of the water-chestnut.

Within it, the seat where the empirical consciousness dissolves has the cognitive energy for support. But as long as one identifies the bodily

8. *Amedhya.*

9. Probably the sixteen *ādhāra* mentioned by Gorakṣanātha in *S.S.P.* ch 2 śl. 11 to 25: (1) *pādāṅguṣṭha* (the big toe), (2) *mūlādhāra,* (3) *gudādhāra* (with anus contraction and expansion), the place of *apānavāyus,* (4) *medhrādhāra,* the sex organ, (5) bladder, (6) navel, (7) heart, (8) throat, (9) uvula (*ghaṇṭikā*), (10) *tālu,* (11) the tongue, (12) *bhrūmadhya,* (13) *nāsādhāra,* where the mind becomes steady, (14) *nāsāmūla,* root of the nose, (15) *lalāṭa,* forehead, and (16) *brahmarandhra,* wherein the *ākāśacakra* resides.

tie with consciousness, one keeps on wandering in the triple world.

So, adorned with the three energies, the supreme Self (*paramātma*) remains the same—the mirror of absolute Consciousness wherein the universe is reflected. Skilled in perceiving the activities of becoming, it is endowed with manifold modalities and energies when, assuming the state of the sleep [of ignorance], it is perceived as the moon reflected in water. And yet, this is Maheśvara, all-pervading Lord, creator of the fourteen species of beings—He, the supreme Self."

Analysis

The purpose of this treatise is to show how the supreme Self, adorned with the three major energies—will, knowledge, and activity (*icchā, jñāna,* and *kriyā*)—lies dormant in the human body in the form of Kuṇḍalinī and how it reveals itself.

Gorakṣa's description of the centers is both cryptic and minute, for he perceives in one complete overview all the effects of the piercing; thus, instead of a single perspective, a new complexity is offered at every stage. This pattern of the work probably reflects as much the spontaneous and all-encompassing nature of the Nātha's experience as a deliberate esoteric intent.

The sense of the allusions can be explained and clarified, but such an analysis cannot be free of linguistic technicalities.

Between the center that shuts and opens the anus and the sex organ, a triangle, in the middle of the *mūlādhāra,* is inscribed within the three circles of this *maṇḍala.* At each corner of the triangle, there is a knot and in the center of those knots a lotus with four petals, turned downward in one who is engaged in worldly activities and upward in one who turns away from them.

In the lotus pericarp Kuṇḍalinī lies coiled; she is called a conch (*śaṅkhinī*) because of her being folded three and a half times. Red like a young coral sprig, she appears in the form of two or three currents, the seeds of which will develop as *iḍā* and *piṅgalā,* the third being *suṣumnā.* Just like a sprout latent in its seed,

Kuṇḍalinī lies dormant, hence the expression "seed of consciousness," as the latter, still obscured, has to be awakened.

From the bulb *(kanda)* spring the 72,000 currents, including the two well-known *iḍā* and *piṅgalā nāḍī*. Six pathways come out of the navel (*nābhi*) as Kuṇḍalinī rises: breath, thought, sun,[10] life, and also the fundamental sound from which the ten inner sounds originate,[11] finally the syllables of the *mātṛkā* seated in the lotus centers.

Kuṇḍalinī, as thin as a spider's thread, dwells in the middle of a triple path at the base of the three chief currents, which are released when she stretches up toward the navel.

How can she be made to leave the bulb and pierce the *brahmadaṇḍa*, the median way? By means, we are told, of the bulb staff, namely as a result of the anal contractions and under the action of the breaths known as "bearers of the staff." When beaten by them, the coiled-up energy starts spinning and whirls up from the bulb to the navel. She is thus sinuous and endowed with eight coils (*kuṇḍala*), whose names are already known to us: *praṇava*, *gudanālā* (anus stem), *nālinī* (lotus stem), *sarpiṇī* (the serpentine), *vaṅkanālī* (stem curling backward), *kṣayā* (the one leading to destruction), *śaurī* (pertaining to heroes), and *kuṇḍalī* (the coiled one).

This spiralling upward may generate troubles, depression and cause jerking, all of which cease once the fully-awakened Kuṇḍalinī begins to move upward. Then she reaches the navel whence spring the ten chief currents;[12] *iḍā* or *somanāḍī* is on the left and *piṇgalā* or *sūryanāḍī* on the right; the moon fills the left side of the body and the sun the right side. *Suṣumnā*, or fire, rises in the middle, between them. *Sarasvatī* and *kuhū* are on either side of the median way; *gāndhārī* and *hastijihvā* on either side of *iḍā*, toward the front. Between *gāndhārī* and *sarasvatī* resides *śankhinī*, filled with nectar and extending from the throat to the forehead along a curved line. All these ways have the median way as their main branch.

Thus made up of numerous *nāḍī*, Kuṇḍalinī abides in the "vortex of *brahman*;" indeed, if she were not spinning she could not perform the function of these various vital currents.

10. *Tarpaṇa*, that which heats and burns, should not be confused with *sūrya*, the sun, a symbol of *piṅgalā*.

11. Cf. here p. 153.

12. Enumerated here p. 124.

The navel contains the bearer of the raised staff—the fire that burns upward; through the intense heat released, Kuṇḍalinī becomes firm, erect, as straight as a staff.

Kuṇḍalinī, lower as she is in *mūlādhāra (adhaḥkuṇḍalinī)*, converts into intermediate energy in the navel, then into subtle energy in the heart, in the *anāhata* center, and in the throat (*viśuddhicakra*), and finally into superior energy (*ūrdhvakuṇḍalinī*) when she reaches the *brahmarandhra.*

As the ascent progresses the centers light up: the breath (*pavana*), now purified, illuminates the median way; the mind (*manas*), now omniscient, reveals the effulgence of the supreme Self; the sun (*tapana*) makes the navel and eyebrows' centers shine; Life (*jīva*), at first illumined by the rays of Kuṇḍalinī, in its turn illuminates the heart; finally, sound (*śabda*) together with the mother of the phonemes (*mātṛkā*) cast their light on the *brahmarandhra*.

The description of the various *cakra* from the navel up to the center between the eyebrows, or center of command, does not require much elucidation. This is a clear and classic text. But such is not the case with the superior center.

The *bindu,* a point of concentrated power representing virility and situated above the center between the eyebrows, explodes and expands, thus giving birth to the *mastaka* or *brahmarandhra.* The orifice at the base of the *liṅga,* shaped like a small bell (*ghaṇṭikā*), is the *rājadanta* or elephant tusk; this is also the aperture of the *śaṅkhinīnāḍī.* If the *brahmarandhra* is compared to an elephant tusk, is this because of its ivory hue, or is it to suggest a powerful piercing?

The braincase contains three circles: the fire, sun, and moon *maṇḍala.* In the middle of the latter, *somamaṇḍala,* a stream of nectar, released by the rupture of the *liṅga,* starts to pour into the cranium; then the *śaṅkhinī,* whose tenth door opens into the thousand-petalled lotus (the *sahasrāra*), draws this nectar from the moon circle, and gaining control over it, infuses it into the median way. Then the yogin assumes the *khecarīmudrā* attitude: his mouth half opens of its own accord and he is swept up in full bliss.

Certain Nātha texts give the following details about this attitude: By contracting the throat, the flow of both *nāḍī* (*iḍā* and *piṅgalā*) is brought to a stop therein, and when pressing the tongue [against the uvula], the sixteenth *kalā* moves upward to the place of the triangle (*trikūṭa*), the three-pointed thunderbolt, the syllable *OṂ*.

Or again, according to the *Siddhasiddhāntapaddhati*:[13] "If the yogin meditates on the *kalā*, nectar drips from the moon. Then, curling his tongue back in the *khecarīmudrā* attitude, he prevents this nectar from falling into the destructive fire of the navel region. Accordingly, he attains immortality."

The same treatise further states that what draws the *śaṇkhinī* upward is the spontaneous bliss (56).

And in *śloka* 62: "Through which stem (*mala*) is the liquor [Śiva] extracted and how can the soul drink of it? The nectar collects in the *śaṅkhinī* canal, and the individual soul dwelling in the median way drinks the liquor (*rasa*) through this stem, once it resides in the *mātṛkā*, the whole set of mystic phonemes."

When Kuṇḍalinī awakens, the empirical consciousness first becomes appeased in the heart center; then, on reaching the *brahmarandhra*, it dissolves therein completely (*cittalaya*), to give way to the energy of knowledge (*jñānaśakti*) which leads to absolute Consciousness.

At the same time, the Self hitherto dormant in the lower center, where it was engrossed in the sleep of ignorance and wandering from birth to birth because of its total identification with the bodily bond, now recognizes itself as the supreme Self.

Although it assumed the form of the three energies of will, knowledge and activity, unfolding the latter in this world, and although it has the capacity of discerning the modalities of becoming, the Self remains the Self, and those same energies make it resplendent. According to the traditional analogy, whether it reveals itself as the ultimate Consciousness, a pure mirror wherein the entire universe is reflected, or conversely shows itself as a reflection on this mirror like the moon in water—many moons, distorted and trembling, shimmer in disturbed water, while a single moon, clearly visible and immobile, appears in still water—there is only one and the same mirror, one and the same Self.

13. II p. 3, in Kalyani Mallik's ed., op. cit. here p. 124.

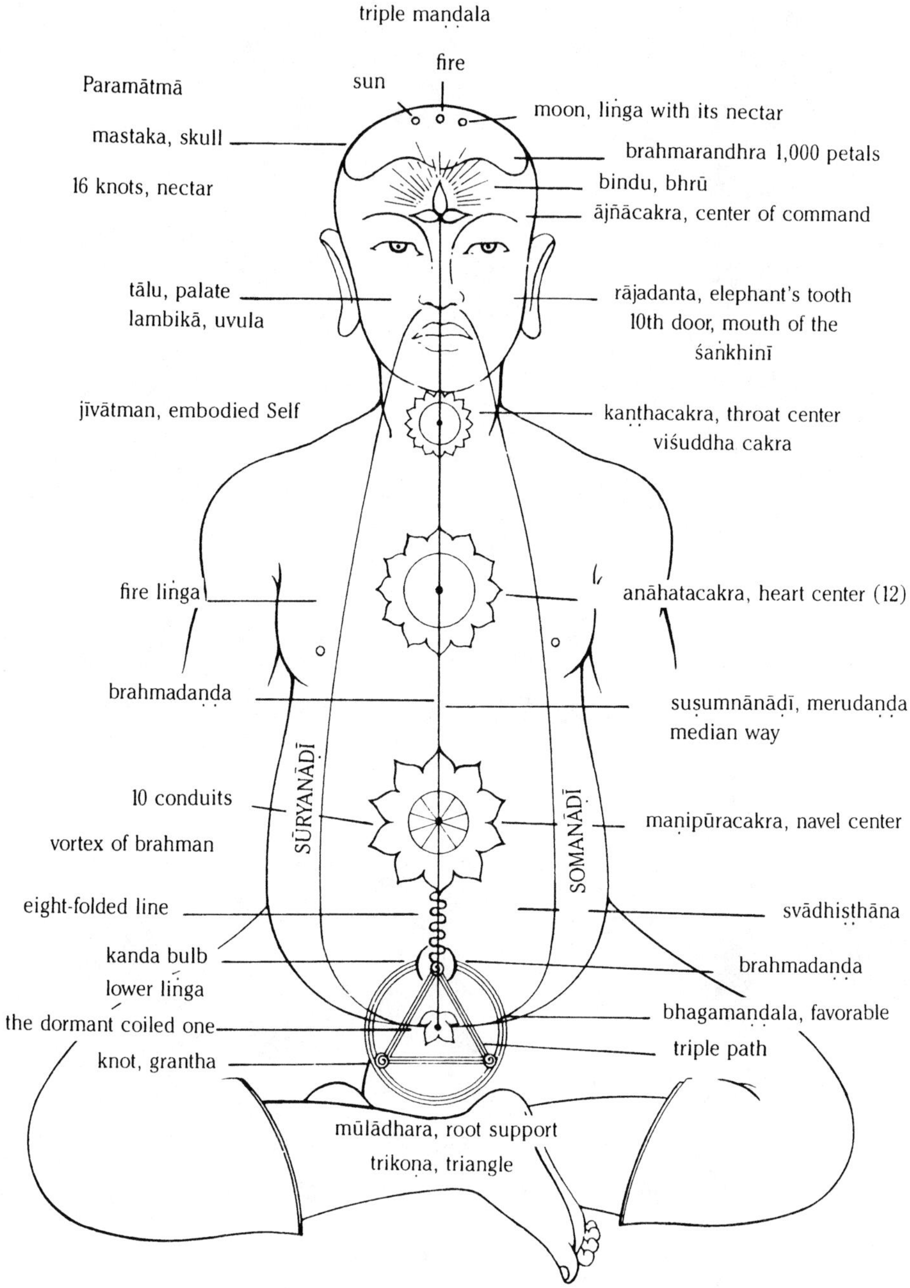
triple maṇḍala
fire
sun
Paramātmā
moon, liṅga with its nectar
mastaka, skull
brahmarandhra 1,000 petals
16 knots, nectar
bindu, bhrū
ājñācakra, center of command
tālu, palate
lambikā, uvula
rājadanta, elephant's tooth
10th door, mouth of the
śaṅkhinī
jīvātman, embodied Self
kaṇṭhacakra, throat center
viśuddha cakra
fire liṅga
anāhatacakra, heart center (12)
brahmadaṇḍa
suṣumnānāḍī, merudaṇḍa
median way
SŪRYANĀḌĪ
SOMANĀḌĪ
10 conduits
vortex of brahman
maṇipūracakra, navel center
eight-folded line
svādhiṣṭhāna
kanda bulb
lower liṅga
brahmadaṇḍa
the dormant coiled one
bhagamaṇḍala, favorable
knot, grantha
triple path
mūlādhara, root support
trikoṇa, triangle

Part Three

THE DEEPER MEANING OF THE ESOTERIC PRACTICE

Chapter One

The Androgyne, *Ardhanārīśvara*

The representation of Śiva as a hermaphrodite, *ardhavīra*, is a favorite one in Indian iconography, the right side of the body being masculine and the left, feminine. Thereby is expressed in a concrete form the free, independent divine energy, as the presence of both sexes in a single body reconstitutes the original oneness of the opposite principles dividing the universe: "Śiva puts his seal upon the whole world," says Utpaladeva, "dividing humanity into male and female bodies"—fragmented parts of one Whole (S.st. XIV.12).

To the *yogin* and *yoginī* who long to recover the fullness of the primordial unity, the way of esoteric sexual union is offered. If they are able to meet its requirements, this union will become a means for them to regain their own wholeness, to inseparably fuse the male and female polarities within themselves—such oneness abiding in seed form in every human being[1]—and to move forever beyond duality.

The sexual union hereafter described is called *rudrayāmala* or the inseparable couple formed by Śiva and his energy. At the time of sexual union, taking advantage of the impetus generated thereby, the adept becomes absorbed in the power of its energy;

1. According to the *Śāktavijñāna*, the root center contains both sexes. Cf. here p. 106.

since consciousness and energy are one, he gains access to the cosmic level of Consciousness and merges, just like the divine pair, into the undifferentiation of the primordial Whole, into Paramaśiva.

Tantrism thus shows how the supreme experience encompasses all the levels of reality, how oneness suddenly arises in the very midst of duality. In Tantrism, indeed, unification must be achieved in the course of ordinary life experiences, whatever they may be; and through the purification brought about by Kuṇḍalinī, any energy may be converted into an energy of pure Consciousness.

Kuṇḍalinī and Sexual Life

Actually, the gap between the energy of pure Consciousness and sexuality remains unbridgeable as long as the "sinuous-bodied" Kuṇḍalinī lies motionless in the ordinary human being. But let the serpentine draw herself up, and the body, permeated with power, becomes the place and privileged instrument for the attainment of Bhairavian Consciousness, providing, it is true, that the yogin joins mystical discrimination to renunciation, just as the swan skillfully extracts from the cosmic waters the quintessential juice of Consciousness.[2]

Any form of pleasure gives a glimpse of the bliss of the Self; for when desire has been fulfilled one rests within oneself; but this does not mean that the actual Self has been revealed in its fullness.

If, when Kuṇḍalinī becomes erect and the energies are purified, pleasure is used as a stepping stone, it converts into the bliss of pure Consciousness. So, the sexual rite through which access to cosmic Consciousness is to be gained rests upon the specifics of sexual union, such as touch, fervor and bodily satisfaction, and it raises pleasure to its climax, transmuting it into a calm and unbroken bliss, as the polarity of desire can give way to the delight of the Self.

Touch

Among the five senses, touch, to which the sexual organs are related, is given a special place; as it is of a more intimate nature

2. Cf. here p. 146.

than the other senses, it facilitates contact with the median way,[3] and thus awakens it; on the other hand, it is linked to an overall emotion which brings about the quick unification of the naturally dispersed tendencies and leads to the fulfillment of desire.

Abhinavagupta quotes a stanza from the *Spandakārikā* (III.10) to show how touch was highly regarded by his predecessors who do not mention it among the obstacles to *samādhi*, such as strange luminous dots, smells, savors and sounds arising unexpectedly as a result of a deep absorption; he himself further states (T.A. XI 29–33): "The organs of sight, hearing, taste and smell are subtly present in earth and the other elements belonging to lower levels of reality, the highest among them being still within the sphere of illusion (*māyātattva*), whereas touch resides at the superior level of energy as an indescribable, subtle sensation ceaselessly yearned for by the yogin; for this contact leads to a consciousness[4] identical with the self-luminous, pure firmament."

Jayaratha compares this indescribable sensation (*sparśa*) to a tingle (*pipīlikā*); we know it as an extremely subtle "touch" of divine energy, the very touch of grace.[5]

Effervescence and Fervor

The importance of touch in *kulayāga* must be associated with that of desire the intensity of which provides a valuable support. While sexual desire involves a redoubtable and vain attachment, its intensity, though, remains necessary, nay, essential, because of the lively effervescence it stirs up. In esoteric union, in

3. *Madhyamacakra,* cf. here p. 172.

4. Here three terms refer to consciousness: *saṃvitti*, *cit*, and *prakāśa*.

5. Some Upaniṣad had already established a correspondence between touch, *udāna* breath (or Kuṇḍalinī), and zenith. The Chāndogya, when dealing with the five channels, sets the equivalence between the upward-flowing channel or *udāna* and the wind and the *ākāśa*; the latter is the inner space in a human being, within the heart; and this *ākāśa*, which is plenitude and immutability, is not different from the outer space identical with *brahman* (III.13.5 and 12.7–9). And as for the zenith, which because of its overhead position is suggestive of the ascendant breath, *udāna*, it states again: "Brahman feeds on the *brahman* flower from which the Upaniṣad bee (the science of mystical correspondences) gathers honey in the beehive of heaven, at the zenith, where the sun—a symbol of *brahman*—is the honey of the gods, while the combs are the zenith rays."

fact, bodily effervescence, when free from attachment,[6] supplies a basis for the unfoldment of mystical fervor.

If, disengaged from amorous possessiveness, *kāma*, the god of desire, consumed by Śiva's third eye—the Kuṇḍalinī energy—gives way to amorous tenderness[7] nourished by reverence, or if, beyond knowledge and known, desire changes into a pure outflow of impersonal love (*icchā*), its bare intensity energizes the body and the latter, free from individual limitations, functions unimpeded, so that the yogin can stand at the source of energy, in the vivid impression of the first glimpse.

Avoiding the duality of choice and objectivity, the awakened senses freely unfold their activity in an impersonal manner; as the body is thus satisfied, the yogin gains access to cosmic bliss. This is why the *Vijñānabhairavatantra* recommends: "Let the thought, which is now mere delight, be fixed on the interval between fire and poison.[8] [Then] it becomes isolated or filled with breath and [one merges] into the bliss of love" (śl.68).

It goes on to state: "The enjoyment of the Reality of *brahman* [experienced] when absorption in the energy, vigorously stirred through union with a consort [*Śakti*], comes to an end, that is known as intimate enjoyment" (69).

When the bliss related to sensual pleasure permeates the entire being and changes into intimate mystical enjoyment, it transcends desire and purifies thought, which it calms down.

So, according to the great saying of the Tantra, that which is a cause for bondage to ordinary humans proves to be, to the *siddha*, a means of liberation. Even in the height of the agitation particular to sexual desire, one is carried, through the ascent of Kuṇḍalinī, to where the energy surges forth, to its vibrant source. That is the secret behind profound Tantra such as the *Parātriṃśikā*, a secret revealed by Abhinavagupta in his gloss thereon.[9]

So, as an instrument of realization, the body takes on a special value, for once the energies have crossed the boundaries of the individual, they pervade the universe and as such they are called "divinities."[10]

6. *Rāga*.
7. *Rati*.
8. Cf. here p. 52. The technical terms fire (*vahni*) and poison (*viṣa*) refer respectively to the beginning and end of the sexual act, and on another level, to the contraction and expansion of energy during the ascent of Kuṇḍalinī.
9. P. 50.
10. *Devatā*, a term already used in the earliest Upaniṣad.

Abhinavagupta says in this connection:

> "All the things flung with great force into the fire burning within our own consciousness lose their differentiation while feeding its flame with their own energy. As soon as the nature of things has dissolved in this speedy burning process, the divinities of consciousness—the rulers of the sense organs—delight in the universe now turned into nectar. Now satisfied, they identify Bhairava to themselves, Bhairava, firmament of Consciousness, God dwelling in the Heart, He, perfect plenitude."[11]

According to the gloss, the divinities become aware of the universe as a reflection within the supreme Consciousness. The conscious subject and the object it revels in are likewise interrelated, for the divinities, although resting in the undifferentiated, have varied functions and activities in connection with the different sense organs turned toward their respective objects.

11. T.A. III 262–264.

Chapter Two

Transfiguration of the Body and of the Universe

So that one may better understand the nature of the contact between subject and object, the Self and the other, Abhinavagupta quotes an obscure passage from the *Yogasaṃcara*.[1]

Although it seems to stress sexual contact, since the latter is the most intense of all, this text is also concerned with any relationship between an organ and its specific object.[2]

But rather than a mere contact, this is intimate union (*mithuna*) with a background of joy, in one with an awakened heart. The repeated friction between subject and object quickens the interchange and ends in fusion. Without such a friction the object remains limited and the subject does not gain access to the universal nectar. But through this friction, which induces the intensification of joy and energy, the delineations of the object dissolve and the subject/object duality ceases.

So through the unification of two poles, friction may be for the yogin an opportunity to merge into the Whole, he enjoys cosmic Consciousness, body and universe being transfigured.

1. T.A. IV 130–146, in the light of Jayaratha's commentary, p. 138 seq. which also inspires my own analysis.

2. One who exerts an intense vigilance may experience subject-object interpenetration during any type of union, such as between two waves of knowledge, between two sounds, for instance. It is to this type of all-inclusive experience that nondualistic Śaivism owes its universality.

146. Consciousness, being free, reveals itself as both inner reality and outer reality, while still being of the nature of Self-awareness.

130. It becomes manifest in three successive spheres: subject or fire, knowledge or sun, and known or moon. In the intimate union (*mithuna*) of fire and moon, a reciprocal exchange takes place through contraction and expansion.[3] From this unifying friction of subject and object arises plenary Consciousness.

131. Just as, when joining, *yoni* and *liṅga* emit ambrosia, in the same way, out of the union of fire and moon flows ambrosia; there is no doubt about this.

The part played by *agni* and *soma* in the Vedic rite may throw some light on this excerpt. The sacrificial fire rises straight in the firmament to carry to the gods all the offerings it has consumed. Setting heaven and earth apart, it gives birth to a new dimension. Likewise, the fire of Kuṇḍalinī consumes all multiplicity and brings it back to its essence of undifferentiated Consciousness when, gaining access to the supreme firmament—the *brahmarandhra*—it loses itself in its immensity.

As for the *soma* plant, squeezed between the sacrificial stones and then purified, it yields its inebriating sap to the divinities. The moon (*soma*) appears in the Āgama as the symbol of the known which, illumined by the sun of knowledge (*sūrya*) and squeezed by the subject (*agni*), pours out its nectar enjoyed by the divinities that are the transfigured organs.

Kuṇḍalinī appears thus prefigured in the intense heat of *agni*, the brilliance of the sun and the nectar of immortality (*amṛta*).

132–133. In the depth of night [which are the ordinary activities] steeped in illusion, both wheels—subject and object—must be strongly pressed so that their sap be extracted. From their interpenetration flashes forth at once an eminent splendor, that of the supreme Knower exceeding

3. *Sammīlana* and *unmīlana*.

in brightness the sun and the moon [knowledge and known].

As soon as [the yogin] knows this supreme light—his own Self—then he knows *Bhairava*, the universal cause, perfect light of Consciousness or supreme Subject. Such is the Knowledge of the ultimate Reality.

133. Indeed, beyond the two wheels of subject and object there is a thousand-spoked wheel, the *sahasrāra*,[4] the universal Consciousness from which the universe proceeds.

134–136. When the supreme Subject, or fire, sets the object ablaze—the moon [that is to say the energy at work in this world, *kriyāśakti*]—the latter releases the flow it contains and engenders the world common to all humans, as well as the varied world specific to each individual.

Then this energy,[5] all ablaze, pours its supreme nectar on all sides, right into the wheel of the subject, through the wheel of the object and that of knowledge; and this nectar trickling from wheel to wheel finally reaches the fivefold wheel [namely the body and its subtle organs, intellect, thought, etc.]

In other words, the objective energy streams from wheel to wheel not, as might be inferred, from the superior wheel of the Subject down to the inferior wheel of the objective world, but from the latter up to the wheel of the Subject; and thence it flows back to the outside—the body and its sense organs.

Once it has regained its true nature, *soma* melts into the universal center, then, in its turn, it emits the universe inwardly, when the generic vibration arises.

The supreme Subject then discovers within himself the "secret" wheel, so-called because it is related to sexual union. It orig-

4. Cf. here p. 31.

5. *Soma*, the transfigured object, pours ambrosia as does the sixteenth portion of the moon when the other portions merge one after the other into the sun, namely the ascendant breath (*udāna*). Cf. T.A. VI.96–97.

inates from the eminently creative birthplace,[6] the seat of bliss or pleasure. Three levels can be distinguished there: the cosmic level which, as it is related to the supreme Subject, brings forth and withdraws the world in a joyful play; the individual level, which is for each man the seat of the pleasure he is attached to; lastly, the mystical level, the place of the so-called bliss of *brahman*, the special attribute of the yogin known as *brahmacārin* who, discovering this secret wheel in the very midst of *samādhi*, harmonizes bliss in this world with rest in the Self.

With the wheel of resorption peculiar to the universal Subject, everything once again becomes interiorized: the flow of the sublimated objective energy courses harmoniously and the Subject enjoys the universe with discrimination, just as the swan skillfully extracts from the cosmic waters the sap of Consciousness.

> 136. The swan[7] of dazzling whiteness drinks the world (*idam*) again and says with immense joy: "I am That" (*haṃ-sa*).

Thus becoming aware of the Self as universal Subject, it resorbs everything within itself and becomes thereby fully satisfied:

> 137. Only once does he have to realize his identity with the world, and never again will he be defiled by merits and demerits.

Then the Subject goes toward the world and as the flow pours outside, the innermost essence spreads out as transfigured exteriority during the sexual practice described in the next verses:

> 137–138. This omnipresent [swan]—the su-

6. *Janmasthāna*.

7. *Haṃsa*. These stanzas shed light on some other famous lines from the *Maitry Upaniṣad* (V.34): "This golden bird which rests in the heart and in the sun (*āditya*), the swan of unequalled splendor, in fire must it be honored." Is not this bird the supreme Subject, the Self? Indeed, the Upaniṣad enjoins one to meditate on this splendor of *Savitṛ* as the very splendor of the meditating subject. Then, reaching the haven of peace, one becomes firmly rooted in the Self. Cf. here p. 88, an allusion to the sacrificial fire, *agnihotra*, which, however, is conceived of in this Upaniṣad as an inner fire that should be honored for its purity.

preme Self—that, out of mere freedom associates with changing modalities in the five-spoked wheel—the field of the senses—by means of the nectar flowing from the transfigured world (*soma*), glides toward the secret wheels with their threefold spoke of savor. From there, the universe originates, as the expression of his free play, and there also does it dissolve.[8]

139. Therein lies beatitude for all and therein again the *brahmacārin* giving himself with ardor to *brahman*[9] achieves, owing to this secret wheel, both efficience in this world and liberation.

Brahmacarati, "he moves toward *brahman*," and accordingly appears as identical with the supreme *brahman* made of pure bliss:

140. Then, beyond this secret wheel—the wheel of birth—he finally gains access to the realm of *brahman*, where subject and object, being in harmony, are emitted within the Self and by the Self.

"By the Self," "*haṃsa*," the swan, and "within the Self," namely *Parameśvara*, this pure mirror wherein are reflected subjectivity and objectivity, *agni* and *soma*.

So, as Kuṇḍalinī rises, the yogin reaches, beyond the wheel of birth, the superior center (*brahmarandhra*), and there does he lay the creative seed; he enjoys the Brahmic state where interiority and exteriority are balanced and henceforth undifferentiated. And in so doing he brings forth the universe, which would be impossible should he plant this seed in objectivity alone.

The next stanzas describe the ebb and flow of the subjective and objective energies as one predominates over the other. If the outwardly-turned activity prevails, the world appears:

8. Not only on the individual level but also on the level of the appeased Self.

9. About the bliss of *brahman*, cf. V.B. appendix p. 195.

141. *Soma*—divinized object—which in this realm is in harmony with the subject, having begotten the universe within, brings it into outer manifestation, down to the earth, if, well-kindled by fire (the Subject), it permeates in a two-fold way as far as the legs.

But when the subject reigns supreme, the activity energized by its flame reaches its climax and the *prāṇakuṇḍalinī* energy[10] is clearly felt inside the body.

141–142. If the Subject predominates over the object, ambrosia immediately begins to flow. Then this energy in the form of activity, made of *soma* [transfigured object] and illumined by the sun [knowledge] of *prāṇakuṇḍalinī*, manifests clearly in the ankles, the knees, and the other joints. She is the one who, further excited by fire [the Subject], sends forth successively the five sense rays.

143. Let this process be also witnessed in the sense organs such as the ears, and the organs of action down to the feet, in regard to the body as composed of five elements,[11] from the big toe up to the vision of the egg of *brahman* [the *brahmarandhra* or, according to the gloss, the "world" enclosed therein].

144. He who is unaware of this is not a yogin; he who knows it becomes the master of the universe . . .

147. So Consciousness manifests as both internal and external reality; and there, within its own Self, due to its own freedom, it appears as

10. *Kuṭila*, glossed as *prāṇakuṇḍalinī* on p. 127.

11. At the same time the body and the universe made up of the same elements—earth, water, fire, air—manifest externally, for the supreme Consciousness not only dwells in the sense organs and the organs of cognition, but also in the constituent energies of the external world.

the "other",[12] in the aspect of subject and object.

From these stanzas, which Abhinavagupta deliberately made obscure, their contents being, he says, too secret to be revealed (146), it may be inferred that the outward-directed activities attain a state of harmony—equality of subject and object—through Kuṇḍalinī alone and not without her. As we shall see, the purpose of sexual practice is to infuse the interiorized state of *samādhi* into the so-called outer sphere, and thence into the inner one again; thereby, in any state perfect harmony is experienced. When interiority invades the various domains, life and activity reach their apogee, Kuṇḍalinī's ascent having made the purified energies of the yogin converge toward the single center—thus revealing a renovated world where his divinized energies[13] unfold.

What other form of adoration can there be but that of a Heart containing everything within itself?

12. "The other" is *māyā*, the illusion, which nevertheless resides within the conscious oneness.

13. The twelve *kālī* of the Krama system. On this topic see *Hymnes aux kālī*, chapter III, p. 40 seq. and 153–190, and T.A. IV 148–173, p. 157–206.

Chapter Three

The Mantra SAUḤ and KHA

Abhinavagupta[1] gives some illuminating comments on the subject of divine nectar, that realm of happiness[2] filled with the flow of an emission won over by a yogin who remains carefully aware of the vibration of the bliss conduits, that is, the *nāḍī* of the united couple, and this means both the unifying friction of Śiva and the energy whence cosmic bliss surges, and the union of the *siddha* and the *yoginī* through which this state is revealed.

SAUḤ. The Mantra of Emanation

Abhinavagupta associates this supreme nectar with the *parabīja SAUḤ*, symbol of the nectar of immortality produced by the cosmic sacrifice where the universe, in the form of a moon,[3] serves as an oblation thrown into the fire of Consciousness. A paradox indeed, it is by emitting in the fire (or supreme Subject) the conscious nectar—Life-source or *S*—that the universe, even though it is exterior, brings about increased interiority.

1. T.A. V. śl 62 to 73, abridged.
2. *Saudabhūmi*.
3. The universe is called moon, *soma*, when conceived as divine Energy—the virgin Umā united to Śiva (*sa* + *umā* = *soma*).

Then, this divine nectar, like clarified butter, on reaching the tapered end of the sacrificial ladel—or *AU*—the trident of energies, spreads as far as mundane activities, so that all the organs are perfectly satisfied.

Finally the two points of the *visarga* (*Ḥ*)—external and internal—unified in a single point (the *bindu*) reveal the nectar of the *visarga*, that is, the "release" of the supreme current flowing into the fire of Consciousness. At that moment, there is no longer any difference between the flowing of this nectar in our own essence and its flowing in a universe pervaded by Consciousness. There, in the Heart of the *yoginī*, the fully aware being, now able to rest there forever, attains glory itself.

Abhinavagupta finally declares that the working of *SAUḤ* in the fire of consciousness, as related to the beatitude of emission, remains in deep secrecy and should not be given any form of elucidation.

Later on, however (śl 142–145), he again comments on the meaning of *SAUḤ* in sexual practice, when dealing with the spontaneous sound—the self-existent, very subtle and omnipresent *dhvani*, which must be realized through direct experience. Although non-manifested, this pure resonance can be traced in the amorous cry (*sītkāra*), unintentional and unrelated to concentration, spontaneously arising from the throat of the woman absorbed in the pleasure of love.[4]

This simple resonance (*nādamātra*) is "a desire whose reality is plenary essence."[5]

One-pointed on this amorous cry, the man catches the initial vibration, that of the first stirring of the supreme Consciousness.

Now let us deal with the meaning of the mantra *SAUḤ* in relation to the rising of Kuṇḍalinī.

S is a desire to join with the beloved, without the least personal attachment. It is also the commencement of the contact with the supreme Consciousness, *AU*. Then, during sexual union, when heart, throat, and lips take part in the unfoldment of the whole being, Kuṇḍalinī rises inside the median way through bulb, heart, throat, upper palate, up to the *dvādaśānta*, both lovers remaining aware of the process going on in the median way as pure interiority. Such is the access to the phoneme *AU*, the place of identification,

4. T.A. III 146–148.
5. Ibid., comm. p. 148.

once the lovers become firmly established in the undifferentiated Self.

If the yogin evokes the creative seed *SAUḤ*, fully vibrant with bliss, within the median canal, then he will reach the peerless Consciousness in relation with the supreme *dvādaśānta*.

Ḥ or : When the *visarga*—transcribed by two dots one above the other—is operative in both the internal and external pathways of the *dvādaśānta*, the fully vigilant yogin unites those two *dvādaśānta* with the heart.[6]

Let us add that it is very difficult to obtain the interiorized union during the sexual act particular to this emitting seed,[7] where both lovers are merged in each other; the man must forget about his being a male, as the subjective realm enters the objective realm and vice versa, a necessary condition for the sense of self to vanish.

At the same time, on the universal level, pure being, *sat*, symbolized by *S*, penetrates into *AU*—the three, well-harmonized energies—then the emitting power of Śiva (namely the *visarga Ḥ* of the superior center) unites with the heart. Thus the universe (*Sat*) will be emitted in the heart of Bhairava and attain repose.

KHA. The Mantra of Resorption

Another mantra, *KHA*, related not to creation this time but to resorption, is associated with the rising of Kuṇḍalinī; it too relates to sexual practice and like SAUḤ implies a permanent absorption, even in the midst of the world.

It consists of successive sojourns in ten inner spaces of ever-greater peace. These are the ten *KHA*.[8]

First the yogin contemplates the awakening of Kuṇḍalinī dwelling in the lower center; he utters the mantra *KHA*, and by concentrating on it, infuses it into the energy, while making the power of the mantra rise in the median channel, up to the superior center. Beyond the stages of the two energies—knowledge and activity—as the subject/object duality has dissolved, he reaches the energy of will and then he becomes conscious of the Self (*svavimarśa*). Finally, transcending the Fourth state wherein the dazzling

6. ŚI 142–147. Cf. here p. 30.

7. *Sṛṣṭibīja* as *spandanabīja*, vibrant seed.

8. V.145, while *gagana* means infinity, *Kha* or *khe* refers to the centered, vibrant, and appeased space of the heart. Cf. here p. 8 *gaganaśakti* and *khecarīśakti*, *kha* being the hub of the wheel. Cf. P.T.v. p. 10.

rays of pure Consciousness alone flash forth, the adept identifies with the realm of mantra, the source of their power (V. 90–92).

Here is how Jayaratha (p. 400–402) throws some light—very little, in fact—on Abhinavagupta's text:

> By means of discriminative awareness the yogin, becoming established in *KHA*—the Self—begins by finding access to *KHA*—the glorious freedom particular to sovereignty. And while perceiving his own essence, he stands in *KHA*—the individual (*aṇu*)—owing to his abiding in *KHA*—love enjoyment (*rati*)—and if he stays there with a vigilant heart, he penetrates in *KHA*—the root of the breath energy, the womb, the receptacle[9] where *prāṇakuṇḍalinī* takes birth. Then, leaving aside this energy of the *KHA* breath—peculiar to the median domain (*madhyadhāman*)—he raises *kuṇḍalinīśakti* or *ūrdhvakuṇḍalinī*, which penetrates gradually into the median way up to the *brahmarandhra*.
>
> Then he gains access to *KHA*—the fully-unfolded energy of activity (*kriyāśakti*)—right to the domain of the known. Abiding in *KHA*—the cognitive energy (*jñānaśakti*)—he passes beyond knowledge and known and realizes *KHA*—the energy of will (*icchāśakti*). Thereafter, in the center of *KHA*—pure Self-awareness,[10] free from the limits of subject and object—he resides in *turiya*, the Fourth state, the domain of all-pervading Consciousness. Beyond any state (*turiyātīta*), the organs perform their specific functions within their own domain, the ultimate Reality.

According to verses 92 to 99, this ultimate *KHA*—conscious ether—is the empty and appeased space of the heart,[11] wherein

9. That is, *mūlādhāra, janmādhāra*, and *kulamūla*.
10. *Citi* in its full dynamism.
11. *Hṛdvyoman*.

Consciousness alone shines, its three energies losing themselves in the free divine energy.[12]

There are ten sounds corresponding to the ten *KHA*: the onomatopoeia (*ciñcinī*), the sounds made by a cricket, a conch, a stringed instrument, the wind whistling through the bamboos, cymbals, the rumble of thunder, the crackling of a forest fire.

By-passing those nine sounds and their attendant blisses, let one become absorbed in the tenth, the sound of a powerful drum, the only one through which liberation can be attained (p. 410).

12. *Svātantryaśakti*.

Chapter Four

Kulamārga, The Esoteric Way

Qualifications Required for *kulayāga*

There is a profound wisdom in the background of this esoteric sacrifice, so profound indeed that few are those who understand it, and still fewer those who experiment with it.

The sexual practice mentioned here is not a lewd activity, a craving for enjoyment; it does not aim at pleasure or procreation, but appears as a yoga, a discipline, a sacred act having for its goal the realization of the essence of the Self, the identification with Śiva; as such it is essentially ascribable to heroic behavior.

In fact, you need only enumerate the qualifications required for this practice to measure the difficulty of becoming worthy of it and the degree of heroism it demands.

First of all one should be aware that the *caryākrama* practices to which our texts allude are based of necessity on the awakening of Kuṇḍalinī and on her ascension. If she were not to rouse during union, the practice would be utterly worthless; it would have nothing to do with *caryākrama*, for the upward breath alone (*udāna*), as it rises in the median way, bestows the perfect equipoise indispensable to this sacrifice.

A *vīra* or a *siddha* is one who, controlling his senses and his mind, has overcome doubts and limitations. Endowed with a pure heart, having renounced everything, without the slightest attachment to his partner, to desire or enjoyment, he is fully dedicated to inner life, where he shows his daring and adventurous spirit.

Thus during banquets where wine and meat are in plenty, where carnal union is permitted, he proves able to withdraw in a single instant his thought and senses from the source of excitation; oblivious of pleasure at the very climax of enjoyment, he is engulfed in a bliss known as the bliss of *brahman*.

To become fit for the esoteric way the adept must be initiated by a master belonging to a reliable tradition, Krama, Kula, Śākta, or better still, by a *yoginī* who appears to him in a dream or in *samādhi*, or else by a woman initiate, herself also called *yoginī*, who will act as a master for him.

It is for the *guru* to select the right partner. This union being a mystic one, the *vīra* does not see in his partner a mere human being but reveres her as divine, on a par with a *yoginī* or a goddess, without taking heed of her beauty or caste.

Thus, at the beginning of the *caryāvidhi* ceremony, he pays homage to the woman characterized as Śakti and considered as divine consciousness. One of the Tantra's most original features is this respect granted to woman, the embodiment of Śakti, and without which the practice would be fruitless. The followers of Śaktism, Krama, and Kaula worship Mother Kālī, and unlike ancient Buddhism and orthodox Vedānta, they never consider woman as a cause of degradation for man. According to them, rather, enjoyment rightly understood can lead to liberation. So do they revere and glorify woman in all her different aspects as mother, wife and daughter. In a number of Tantra the divine Energy, Parvatī, imparts the mystical teaching to Śiva, her disciple; and most of these masters initiate especially women in the *caryākrama* practice.[1]

Since all of the necessary qualifications demand of the *sādhaka* that, to "interiority", he adds fervor, boldness and intrepidity, it is clear that an ordinary man cannot gain beneficial access to this practice.

> "For one's own benefit," says Abhinavagupta, "one must be careful to avoid performing the *kula* sacrifice with those who do not know the supreme

1. Cf. here p. 163 T.A. *śl.*XXIX 122-123.

> *brahman*[2], who are deprived of the free play [of the breaths] and given over to greed, drunkenness, anger, attachment and illusion."[3]

Therefore this practice must be kept secret and is disclosed only to a few exceptional beings who have overcome the pulls of pure and impure and long to live fearlessly and intensely, with all their capabilities fully unfolded. Such is the true spirit of the Tantra which grasp life as a whole, without suppression or mutilation, and thereby accord all the vital, emotional, and intellectual tendencies their due place in the making of a free and complete being.

But let it not be misunderstood by the Westerner, he who is not troubled by vain scruples in his pursuit of power. To break away from all restraint is not enough to qualify for *caryākrama*. The adventurer in search of an original life has neither the required purity nor the humility which would allow his surrender to the master. He is too easily deluded with a so-called experience of awakening of his Kuṇḍalinī and about the role that ordinary sexual union can play in this respect. Thus he does not qualify for *kulayāga* because of a double obstacle, one of a technical nature: lack of a master and of knowledge, the other of an inner nature: lack of purity of heart.

Nor is such a course of action suitable to those fond of piety, like certain *brahmin* who are unable to overcome doubts and prejudices, and pronounce a final condemnation of the esoteric practice.

Abhinavagupta points out the serious risks involved for those who take to a practice not meant for them,[4] as the follower of *kulayāga* easily falls a prey to hell if he enjoys forbidden things without being a hero (*vīra*).

But if he is worthy of performing such a rite, he takes part in the meetings of *yoginī* and *siddha*—initiated women and men; on the spiritual plane, those meetings correspond to the union of the *vīra's* divinized energies (*yoginī*) with their sense objects (*siddha*), in other words, the perfect, undifferentiated[5] fusion of knower and known.[6]

2. Namely the bliss derived from the three *M*s. Cf. here p. 163.
3. T.A. śl.289–90, last stanzas of chap. XXIX.
4. T.A. XXIX, 99. Cf. here p. xiii.
5. *Nirvikalpa*.
6. Cf. here p. 167.

Effects of the *Caryākrama* Practice

The heroic practice is focused entirely on the experience of the identity of Śiva and the energy at the completion of Kuṇḍalinī's ascent. But the verticality it brings into play involves a double achievement. First it collects, gathers and unifies all the scattered horizontality which characterizes ordinary existence. Then the acme of this horizontal dimension—sexual life—is transmuted into a pure vertical impetus.

The yogin discovers many benefits in such a unifying practice; it purifies and intensifies the energy; it dissolves doubts and limitations; it enables him to gauge the depth of his renunciation, the true touchstone being that, in the height of union, the couple remains in *samādhi*. Finally, the *kulayāga* is a means for the *siddha* and the *yoginī* to help each other, in that if one of the partners fails to enjoy a permanent awakening, he or she may receive it through the other.

Haven't we said that sexual practice is intended only for the yogin whose heart has already been purified? True, but his thought, body, and organs are not equally pure; and to purify them the energy must be activated, for through the unfolding of any spiritual energy one may regain the purity of the heart impulse. However, mystical excitation and fervor are not easy to achieve; they have nothing to do with the physical, emotional, mental and sensory excitations of ordinary life, among which sexual excitation ranks first. For they are related to the profound fundamental vitality called *ojas*. So, to increase the latter, one should develop a fervor capable of grasping the energy in its first stirring, "just when a spark of the *spanda* flies in the heart" (P.T.v. p.45).

In most of his works and commentaries, Abhinavagupta stresses the intense life or the fervor which stands in contrast with the indifference of those beings whom nothing can move; he does so because Śiva and Śakti—Consciousness and energy—are but one: to awaken the energy is to awaken Consciousness.

The churning of the energy by Bhairava during the creative emission corresponds to an effervescence which spreads as a nectar of eternal bliss, a nectar that Abhinavagupta detects at every level, and even in the union of sexes:

> "Let bliss be experienced," he says, "through the unifying friction of the sexes at the moment of mutual enjoyment; and by its means,

let the unparalleled, ever-present essence be recognized. Indeed, all that enters through an inner or outer organ abides in the form of consciousness or breath in the domain of the median way; the latter, related essentially to the universal breath (*anuprāṇanā*), infuses life to all bodily parts. That is what is called *ojas*, vitality, which energizes the whole body" (P.T.v. p.46–47).

Ojas is the virility that does not flow out of the body, that of the *brahmacārin* for example. *Vīrya*, efficience,[7] is *ojas* manifested through the many aspects of power, whether that of the great formula, the mantra "I", or that of virility proper.

Everything, such as color or sound, may produce in one who is well provided with this power, some effervescence, excitation or stir (*kṣobha*) of the energy, which rouses the fire of desire... however, this is only for a strong virile power, full and rich, not for an incomplete or defective virility as that of a young boy or an old man. When *vīrya* is thus agitated, a sense of freedom is experienced, which is both energy of bliss and plenary Consciousness of Bhairava.

Abhinavagupta then points out that such efficience being identical with the Self, the flood of pleasure[8] induced by freedom converts into an "intense awareness whose vibrant act (*spanda*) is free from time and space limitations." As to those "who have not increased their virile efficacy within and do not leave any room to the pleasure of the god of love, they remain like rocks when facing a beautiful maid and hearing her melodious songs, deprived as they are of inebriation and bliss." For virility and rapture go hand in hand; rapture grows in proportion to virile potency: "Lack of virility," he says, "is lack of life, lack of the power of wonder."

7. Cf notice at the end of the chapter, 176.

8. Not only does this occur in the course of various enjoyments, but right in the midst of pain, provided the emotion is experienced in its true essence and access to universal efficiency is found; then Reality reveals itself in the form of a wonderful unfoldment of the energy.

Sensitivity belongs to one "endowed with heart" (*sahṛdaya*), immersed in fervor, and whose virile potency is agitated, for only the heart fortified by this force is capable of wonder (p.47-49).

Abhinavagupta goes on to show (p.50) how the agitation that shakes the whole being converts into divine energy, when one penetrates into the *Rudra-Rudrā* couple, Śiva and his energy, namely into bliss and plenary emission:

> If one succeeds in becoming one with the efficience of one's own energy, at that very moment Bhairava stands revealed in the immovable domain, provided all the breaths of the sense channels reach their plenitude; then one becomes absorbed in the great domain of the Center, *suṣumnā*, while duality dissolves. So, to penetrate into *suṣumnā* is to penetrate into *rudrayāmala*, to experience the rapture of the supreme interiority and become fully aware of one's own overflowing energy.

Thus during the ascent of Kuṇḍalinī, when the currents unite and one becomes identified with the median way, as the moment of trembling particular to sexual union arises, one can experience the pleasure of an intimate contact consisting in the effervescence of the whole virile potency about to burst forth. Then let one take hold of this power as primordial vibration. Captured at its source, the energy dissolves all limitations and brings about the shift from the individual to the universal. This is why Abhinavagupta explains that the subject matter here is not our limited body but the "I" in the form of the great mantra *AHAM*. In fact, says he, Śiva, the supreme Word, emits the efficience of the great mantra "I" by generating his higher energy through a great influx of his power; and since there is identity between the efficience of word, awareness of the Self, and virility, the power of this mantra makes it possible to gain access to the immovable realm.

The divine emission, which is bliss and freedom, combines the pure Consciousness of Śiva and the efficience of energy.

Uncertainty and Fluctuation (*kaṃpa*)

The most fearful enemies in mystical life are uncertainty, dilemma (*vikalpa*), scruple, doubt, which indicate two conflicting forces and therefore depletion of energy, an obstacle to fervor.

Such is the basic impurity, the contraction of the heart, "a massive bar that blocks the door of the prison known as transmigration." This is why, in the *Bhargaśikharatantra*, the energies of the organs are to be satisfied and propitiated with the help of forbidden substances, and the heroes' vow should be enjoyed (T.A. XII 18–21).

Indeed, for the uprooting of doubt there is nothing like disregarding the three major prohibitions to which the orthodox *brahmacārin* are subjected: meat, alcohol, and sexual union.[9] According to the Tantra, a true *brahmacārin* is one who, on the contrary, indulges in them; he enjoys the pleasures of life while not in bondage to them; for to one who is beyond all desire, enjoyment not pursued for its own sake never turns out to be an obstacle; better still, it is a means of liberation since it can be transmuted, like any manifestation of energy, into spiritual power.

The Kashmirian mystic, Lallā, is not afraid of reproval; she sings:[10]

> Arise, O Lady, set out to make thine offering,
> Bearing in thy hand wine, flesh and cakes:
> If thou know the syllable that is itself
> the Supreme Place.
> Thou [wilt also know that] if thou violate
> the custom, it is all the same. What
> loss is there therein? (10)

Far from being blameworthy, these practices even constitute a worthy offering for the deity, provided that Lady Kuṇḍalinī, united with the *praṇava OṂ*, starts to move and reaches, purified, the summit of her course in the "equal" energy (*samanā*).

9. In Sanskrit these terms begin with an *M*.

10. Here, as in Part One, chap. III, Lallā's verses are given in Sir George Grierson's translation. In his note to *śl.* 77, the translator observes: "The 'violation of custom' is literally 'the left-handed conduct'." The followers of the right hand revere mainly Śiva; the sectarians of the left hand (*vāmacārin*) place more importance on the divine energy (*śakti*) and are concerned mostly with śāktism.

The great sacrifice which aims at unfolding the whole conscious and unconscious personality, helps one to overcome social prejudices, instinctive aversions, obscure and deep-rooted fears, so that only the vibrant energy remains. Then as doubts are radically uprooted, along with the forces of limitation which inhibit the impetus of the whole being, the mystic attains free Bhairava.

One who has been able to observe the countless restraints of Indian life in religious, ritualistic and social matters, a legacy from Vedic orthodoxy, will more easily understand how much a mystic needs to break away from conventions and prohibitions, in particular from those laid down for *brahmacārin*. Intrepidity and virility (*vīrya*) then take on their full meaning.

Living as he was in the midst of innumerable restrictions. Abhinavagupta is all the more admirable for his boldness and independent thinking. He does not hesitate to ridicule the Vedic *ṛṣi*; for, says he, what they regard as degrading is held here as a rapid means of attaining spiritual realizations. Thus it is knowingly, deliberately, so that one may be released from the bondage of ties, that he recommends taking to the three *Ms*, the most despised means. He shows no consideration for those *brahmin* who, caught up in the dilemmas of pure and impure, are unable to perceive all things in one and the same light.[11]

What is the point wondering about which ritual formulas should or should not be recited? Are they not made up of letters, and are these letters not identical with Śiva, he who is untouched by purity or impurity?

The same holds true as regards what should or should not be drunk: Ganges water or wine, those are just liquids which in themselves are neither pure nor impure. Purity and impurity do not constitute the intrinsic nature of things, or else nature could never be transformed or purified. All this should be considered as mere opinions which, applied to things, are born through exercise of the mind, and that mind, in its essence, is pure.

> What is the criterion of purity? asks Abhinavagupta. That alone is pure which is identical to Consciousness, everything else is impure. No distinction between pure and impure exists for

11. T.A. IV. 240–246, XII. 18–21, XV. 170–177.

him who regards the entire universe as identical with Consciousness.

The *kula* sacrifice can serve as a touchstone to ascertain whether one has truly realized the identity between one's own self and the other, and to measure one's own degree of detachment: does the attraction toward woman, regarded as a desirable "object," still subsist? While it is quite easy to seek refuge in oneself in times of sorrow and worry, it is more difficult to abide in perfect equality, without desire or shame during love enjoyment, the field of the strongest attachment and the most overwhelming emotions. If one succeeds therein, all is attained.

Esoteric Gatherings (*yoginīmelaka*)

Through the *kulayāga*, moreover, one becomes eligible for the *yoginīmelaka*,[12] a source of *samādhi* and Knowledge; as this Knowledge is related to the unfolding of consciousness, one can understand why special significance is accorded to these great assemblies "where all the members of the same mystical lineage (*santāna*) commune" and from which those with contracted consciousness are excluded.

Abhinavagupta writes in this regard:

> "The plenary Consciousness which had become contracted owing to differentiation in bodies, etc., can expand again during these gatherings where all the participants reflect one another (in harmonious union). The flow of their activated organs is reflected in the consciousness of each participant as if in so many mirrors; and the organs, all aflame, attain without effort to universal unfoldment. This is why, at those great gatherings, songs, dances, etc. are fully enjoyed by all who attend when, being one and not distinct, they identify with the spectacle; even at the individual level, their consciousness overflowing

12. Esoteric gatherings. T.A. XXVIII, *śl.* 373 to 380. Cf. M.M. p.131–136.

in joy reaches oneness when beholding the dances . . . and delights in universal bliss (371).

"When free from the causes of contraction such as envy, jealousy . . . the unobstructedly expanding Consciousness is known as 'the bliss of the *yoginī*.'

"But if any among the audience does not identify with the ceremony, his consciousness remaining alien and as if full of asperities . . . let him be carefully kept out of the cult circle, for his consciousness, unfit for any identification, is at the source of contraction."

As to the form of religious worship conducive to perfect absorption in this divine essence—Consciousness—the *Parātriṃśikātantra* advises the yogin to worship the Goddess according to his capacities, by offering her flowers and perfumes, to engage in her cult with devotion, and to offer himself (by way of sacrifice) to the Goddess (*śl.*32).

And Abhinavagupta further states in his gloss that, to carry out the true sacrifice, the devotee must offer fragrant flowers which can easily penetrate into his heart. All internal and external substances used for the cult deposit their essence in his heart. But if his capacities are limited, his energies contracted, if the adept has been unable to make the essence of energy his own and is therefore unfit for such a sacrifice, let him perform a complete worship, with the help of the intimate energy capable of unfolding his own essence, while having also recourse to an outer source of energy, that which accompanies the bliss derived from baths, ointments, incense, betel, wine, etc.

The many different means used for this outer sacrifice bring about an intensification of all the energies and raise them to their melting point, so that they may rush into the median way.

So a *vīra* to whom is offered a variety of rare pleasures and whose heart overflows with joy, experiences an energy at once expanded and controlled where it is most perceptible—in the sexual act; this enables him to return to the source of the free divine energy, as instinct converts into a conscious, self-controlled energy.

We have seen that the enjoyment inherent in this surging forth of energy does not belong to the ordinary body. But how can one speak about the intimate joy alluded to by the *Vijñānabhairava* (*śl.*69), characterized as bliss of *brahman* and experienced only by one who is the master of Kuṇḍalinī?

It may burst unexpectedly, without any contact whatsoever, out of the depths of *samādhi*. This is not a joy pertaining to the limited body; it is dimensionless, though including the body and included in the body. All the sense energies are, as it were, caught by the ascending Kuṇḍalinī, then, in a flash, steeped into such intense bliss that the body is unable to bear it more than a few seconds.

The Kula system goes so far as to contend that identification with Paramaśiva and savoring of universal bliss are impossible as long as the sense organs are not satisfied, for every suppressed desire leaves latent residues not easily conquered. We have seen, moreover, that if one becomes absorbed in bodily bliss, one may, under certain conditions, experience the bliss of Self-Consciousness (*cidānanda*), the latter giving rise in its turn to cosmic bliss (*jagadānanda*). These successive phases correspond to the threefold aspect of pervasion.

1. Individual at first, it appears as the fusion of man and woman, partners in sexual union, as the fusion of inside and outside, or else as that of the self and the other. While this "other" is usually conceived of as a privileged object of enjoyment, from now on inner harmony culminates in a perfect balance between the self and the other.

2. Beyond bodily pervasion (*dehavyāpti*), the yogin gains access to Self-pervasion (*ātmavyāpti*), relating to the Fourth state and the discovery of I-ness; however, a trace of enjoyment can still be detected.

3. By means of the esoteric course, this Self-pervasion can turn into divine pervasion (*śivavyāpti*),[13] all things fusing into Paramaśiva. This is *turiyātīta*, beyond the Fourth state, where the divine essence is perceived as all-pervading, in the impure and in bondage as well as in the pure and in liberation: at the heart of this one-savored unity,[14] Self and universe merge into the Whole in perfect harmony.

The yogin then discovers a most wonderful freedom; both partners disappear, and out of an unfathomable void, mysteriously

13. Or into *mahāvyāpti*, the great pervasion.
14. *Sāmarasya*.

connected with the energy, arises universal bliss in the free play of spontaneity.

When the entire life becomes nothing but divine energy (*kula*), the yogin takes his final rest in the great Heart of the *yoginī*. Such is the deep meaning and the finality of the *yoginī melaka*.

We shall see next how this Heart and its bliss[15] can be experienced, first at the beginning of union, when the current of the breaths suddenly flows out, and at the end, when the *samādhi* unfolds without the sense organs losing contact with their objects, and again when the organs revert to pure interiority.

Quiescence and Emergence

This practice is essentially based on the *śāntodita* process, a double polarity of the energy symbolized by the two dots of the *visarga* and keystone of the esoteric course.

Śānta, quiescent state, is the interiority of the Fourth state, the perfect stillness of *samādhi* corresponding to withdrawal into the appeased depths of the Self. Although this state belongs to the individual, both partners must be united and very quiet; for if quiescence manifests when the couple separates, that is not the *śāntodita* practice.

Udita, emergent or awakened state, suggests a start, an impetus, a free act, free because, being devoid of ties, finality or motivation, it is not subject to any determinism. This term also means awakening, as the yogin is apt to respond at once to the slightest impression when he emerges from the depths of the Self and springs forth so as to conquer the surrounding world. The quick succession of *śānta-udita*, of withdrawal into oneself and emergence, follows the rhythm of the sexual act: the woman's state of emergence corresponds to the man's appeased state and vice versa; so when the man emerges with full consciousness and then sinks back within himself, the woman goes deep inside and thereafter emerges, according to an opposing yet complementary movement.

The moment union is achieved, there is no longer interior nor exterior.

Then interiority reigns supreme and the term *udita* assumes

15. *Saudhabhūmi*.

the meaning of *sadodita*, an ever-surging act, beyond duality and nonduality, both quiescent and emergent.

Life is now but a pulsation, in the form of *nimeṣa-unmeṣa*, slumber and awakening, or of *śānta-udita*; this is how it flows along, this is the *visarga*, whose two poles actually are one.

Union comprises several stages which, following alternating appeasements and emergences, take one beyond, to *kaula*, the ultimate Reality.

1. The practice begins with the external emergent state; when the couple unites, as a result of profuse caresses and kisses, *adhaḥkuṇḍalinī* awakes, and the couple goes into *samādhi*. Mystical union then begins to transfigure ordinary union.

2. The couple reaches the second stage, still comparatively external *śāntodita* where the united man and woman, now immersed and now emerging, act separately and each for oneself. If one of the consorts perceives that the other has not reached the emergent state, he must himself remain in this state until inducing it in his partner. What matters is that there should not for a single moment be a loss of contact, either physically or spiritually.

As excitation reaches its climax, there occurs, on the individual level, an initial gathering of the energies, *saṃpuṭīkaraṇa*, along with vigilance and some kind of exertion. This confluence enables one to enter the Central way, when all the secondary centers rush there and unite in *ūrdhvakuṇḍalinī*.

3. Thence originates the third stage, the appeased state (*śānta*) or retirement within oneself, whose peace still remains individual as Kuṇḍalinī has not completed her ascent. Once the couple experiences the appeased state and the revelation of the Self, then, at the end of union arises the unifying friction.[16]

4. During the fourth phase known as *śāntoditarūpa*, man and woman act in conjunction, according to the alternate movement of appeasement and emergence. As a result of the intense excitation of all the organs, the energies once again rush from all sides toward the central wheel, but here, unlike the first *saṃpuṭīkaraṇa*, the eyes are open and the organs, fully awake, remain vigilant in the very midst of absorption (*samādhi*). During this new spontaneous fusion[17] at a higher level than the previous one, the Self is recognized in its universality. In other words, by means of the alternate attitude (*kramamudrā*), which mixes together interior and

16. *Saṃghaṭṭamelāpa*.
17. *Saṃpuṭīkaraṇa*. Textually "encasing." Cf. here p. 33, 185.

exterior,[18] the *samādhi* peculiar to the appeased state permeates the emergent state, leaving no trace of distinction between them.

5. *Kaula*, ultimate Reality. When union comes to an end and *kramamudrāsamatā* is assumed spontaneously owing to an intense mystical fervor (*ucchalatā*), the couple, freed from the sense of ego, lost in wonder, perceive in the emerging act appeased immobility. They have reached what is called the "inner" emergence, universal Consciousness, energy at its height.[19] When unified quiescence and emergence are integrated and then transcended, *kaula* manifests in all its glory as cosmic beatitude.

Caryākrama and *Kramamudrā*

The fusion of both partners at the end of their harmonious intercourse during *caryākrama* appears, because of its spontaneity, as the path of privileged access to the mystic attitude named *kramamudrā*.[20]

An equal progression (*krama*) leads in both cases to the perfect coincidence[21] of the energy and Śiva. Moreover, the alternate phases, following a certain progression, are also similar: inner withdrawal, outer expansion, and, in between, the supreme Reality (*parakaula*) reveals itself as the source and place of their fusion.

At the pinnacle of the spontaneous movements of retraction and expansion, the individual union of man and woman leads to the mystical and universal union known as *bhairavayāmala*, the confluence of Bhairava and Bhairavī, of Consciousness and Energy. Through union with Bhairava, the universe rests in Śiva; then, the next moment, through union with Bhairavī, the universe awakens. This process goes on moment by moment, until the identification of Bhairava and Bhairavī or of the *siddha* and his consort who then reach the inner *liṅga*, through which Consciousness and bliss are disclosed, while Kuṇḍalinī completes her ascent.[22]

The inner *liṅga*[23] (*adhyātmika*) is identical with the heart and

18. *Samādhi* and *vyutthāna*, cf. here p. 187.

19. *Ūrdhvakuṇḍalinī*.

20. Cf. here p. 56, where Abhinavagupta compares the two movements of *kramamudrā* to those of the stomach of a fish (T.A.v. 58).

21. *Samāpatti*. Also referred to as *saṃpuṭīkaraṇa*, encasing, and *rudrayāmala*.

22. *Ūrdhvakuṇḍalinī*.

23. *Liṅga* means symbol or sign. Capable of discerning Consciousness,

the mouth of the *yoginī*; made of vibrations, this is the *liṅga* of energy and mantric efficacy. There, Reality assumes a wonderful savor because it is at once the place of the Self, the place of bliss, the place of the transfigured universe, and the place whence proceeds the *yoginībhū*, a child predestined to an exceptional mystic life.

This *liṅga* is characterized by the union of interiority and exteriority, even in bodily activity. The *Tantrāloka* declares:

> "Beautified by bliss owing to the perfect coincidence of seed and womb,[24] this *liṅga*, heart of the *yoginī*, engenders an indescribable Consciousness" (V.121).

Related to this very heart is the interiorized sexual practice leading to the ultimate Consciousness. Abhinavagupta draws a parallel between the two *visarga* (this word denoting an "outflow" of felicity): an emission peculiar to sexual practice for one, and then a cosmic emission exclusively related to the free divine energy,[25] whose effervescence inside the median way accompanies the gradual manifestation of bliss and finally blossoms into the fully expanded and active energy.

Indeed, once the energy is suffused with bliss, it swells up outwardly and engages in endless emanations and resorptions of the universe, the two poles of the cosmic *visarga*.

And so it is with *caryākrama*: when in the supreme domain the male and female organs (*liṅga* and *yoni* or *vajra* and *padma*)[26] unite, as a result of enjoyment a flow of bliss[27] is released that engenders the world of men and women.

Jayaratha quotes a stanza in this connection:

---

it assumes three aspects: the lower *liṅga*, pertaining to the individual, is manifested; it is worshiped in temples in a concrete form. The intermediate *liṅga*, wherein interiority prevails, is that of the energy; the supreme, non-manifested *liṅga*, that of Śiva, wherein the universe dissolves, is the divine Heart enclosing, undifferentiated, Śiva, the energy, and the individual; beyond, in the indescribable Reality, no "sign" is needed any more for Consciousness to be apprehended; it is there, self-evident, fully unfolded.

24. *Bīja* and *yoni*.

25. *Kaulikīśakti*.

26. T.A.V. 123–124 and commentary.

27. As emission, *visarga*.

> "That which is praised as the source of the universal flow bestowing felicity is called genital organ (*upasthā*), but it has for its essence the median way" (V. p.430).

Abhinavagupta points out the eminent role played here by the flow of bliss:

> "In this domain full of bliss," says he, "that of an ever-surging consciousness, the whole of the divinized organs reside effortlessly" (122).

Resting in the Self, the yogin experiences utmost delight, even in the midst of his worldly activities: "To live in the undifferentiated even while the differentiated is unfolding, such is the sudden clap of thunder, the roaring[28] of a yogin."

This yogin immersed in the Self, enjoys the glory of his fully expanded organs, fit to perform their varied activities, and which, far from hindering the way of the intimate and immediate experience of the Self, are instrumental in the penetration into the ultimate, all-pervading Self.

Madhyacakra and *Anucakra*

We have described the *cakra* of the body, centers of vibrant energy, which form a dynamic, harmonious whole once they are perfectly tuned, and energized by one and the same life current, Kuṇḍalinī.

In *Tantrāloka* chapter XXIX (*śl.* 106), Abhinavagupta deals with other energy centers, the *anucakra*, which are sense organs characterized as secondary when compared to the chief center, *madhyacakra*. Through these *anucakra*, which open out to the external world, the consciousness of the ordinary human being keeps on wandering. The central wheel, as it is not awakened in the ordinary human being, remains sealed to mystical interiority. Now, if for whatever reason it starts to open, this creates a conflict with the secondary centers whose dispersion goes against its permanent awakening. To make things clearer, let us take an example where

28. In the double meaning of *visphūrjita*. Commentary to 126, p.435.

anucakra refers to the contact between the organ of taste and a fruit; usually the pleasure derived from tasting a fruit is not of such intensity as to give momentary access to the main Center. However, if the yogin, while tasting the fruit, rests within himself in the Center, he attains the union known as *rudrayāmala*, for as his secondary centers are not shut off from the main Center, inner and outer commingle, while the median center opens to infinity.

Through the transmission of the mystical lineage, called "mouth of the *yoginī*," we know how to draw into the chief center not only the secondary centers, but also the multiplicity of external objects. The scattered energies suddenly collect in the Center, which expands and fills in its turn the now-divinized organs with its powerful energy. Then, steeped in wonder, Self-Consciousness illumines all things as identical with it.

During this unfolding of the Center, the three *cakra* of radiant energy—heart, *brahmarandhra*, and *yoginīvaktra*—become one.

To understand why the unfolding of the Center is principally related to those three *cakra*, we have to give a synopsis of the connections between the various centers, starting from the origin.

At first, the wheel of universal Consciousness or infinite energy of the boundless domain[29] alone exists. This wheel then generates a first center of energy called main Center, mouth of the *yoginī*, superior domain, or heart of the *yoginī*.[30] From this wheel proceed the heart and also the sexual apertures (*mukha*). Although the field of action of this effulgence becomes more and more reduced, the energy keeps radiating from the median Center. A return to the Center is therefore possible by means of the unifying friction of the two sexual organs, the friction between them first, and their friction with the heart afterwards.

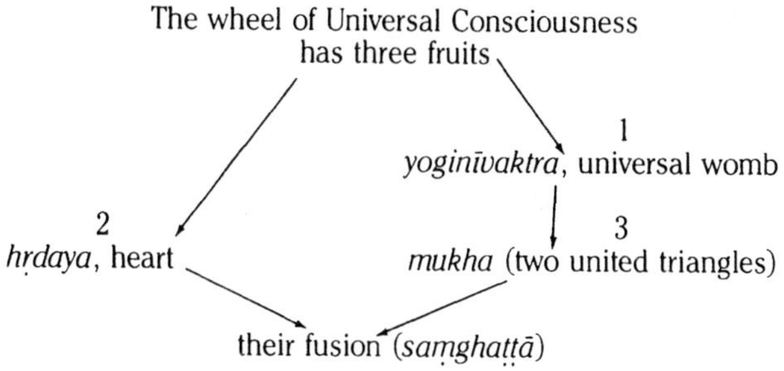

29. *Anavacchinnadhāman*.

30. *Madhyacakra, yoginīvaktra* or *mukhacakra, ūrdhvadhāman*, and *yoginīhṛdaya*.

The fusion of Śiva and Śakti, of the *yoginī* and the *siddha*, is symbolized by two triangles[31] which meet on the completion of Kuṇḍalinī's ascent, when all centers merge in *yoginīvaktra*, and then in universal Consciousness.

The practice of union is therefore related to the domain of the *yoginī*, the universal womb from which everything springs up, while it endlessly expands.[32]

The mouth of the *yoginī* or central wheel affects the heart, vitalizing and activating it, either by extracting from it or by causing its expansion. And during a perfect union between man and woman, it identifies with the heart, *madhyasthāna*. The seat of the heart becomes a universal Center and is no longer distinct from *janmasthāna* and *brahmasthāna*. The *brahmarandhra* fills the womb (*yoni*); and the latter, permeated by consciousness, gives birth to a blessed being.

Such a union is no longer confined to the body, but takes place in the universal domain of the Center (*madhyadhāman*), beyond man-woman differentiation, and also beyond the bodily centers, in the very energy of universal Consciousness, the source of cosmic bliss.

Yoginībhū

For such a union, man and woman must be pure, have no other desire than the divine desire: grace should pervade their whole body; then through an interchange during union, the woman takes in the seed and keeps it in store in the center, this *yoginī*'s mouth, which governs the womb. In the woman there is a substance (*sadbhāva*) which is still purer than the man's *vīrya*, which is the purest element in the human body; when combined with *vīrya*, this substance forms *mahārasa*, a noble and potent essence that controls the development of the child in the mother's womb. It is noteworthy that, while conception occurs at the level of the lower Kuṇḍalinī, it is *ūrdhvakuṇḍalinī* who feeds the embryo.

Yoginībhū, "issued from the inwardly-turned energy,"[33] is the

31. The *ṣaṭkoṇa*, cf. here p. 33.

32. *Yoginīvikāsa*, because of *mahāvyāpti*, cf. here p. 76.

33. According to Abhinavagupta (P.T. *śl.* 10), one must be born of the *yoginī* in order to achieve the ability of perfect absorption in the union of Bhairava and Bhairavī (*yāmalasamāveśa*), and to enjoy the full evidence of the divine Heart.

name given to the child born of a woman who has thus reached a high mystical level. Such was the case, it is said, of Abhinavagupta, conceived by parents who were both absorbed in *samādhi*.

Respective Role of Man and Woman: The *Guru*'s Operation Concerning Them

When a flow of divine energy passes from master to disciple, the latter receives grace and peace effortlessly and sometimes unknowingly. But only a highly experienced *guru* can act upon the heart of his disciple. This heart has two openings; the master, having first closed the outwardly-turned opening, opens the inwardly-turned opening; then from this heart surges forth a torrent which, through the chief *nāḍī*, inundates everything, so that excitation, fervor and the other forms of intensity immediately convert into divine energy. Now the master opens the aperture towards the world and the disciple, while bathing in the peace of the Self, pours it outside. Gradually the disciple in his turn gains control over the opening and closing processes.

Vīrya predominates in man and *prāṇa* in woman. So the *guru* acts upon man's virile efficacy, the essence of semen, to take it up to the *brahmarandhra*; this cannot be achieved without much difficulty, for man's *nāḍī* are narrow, rigid, and not easy to expand; when this essence reaches the superior center, the eyes sparkle like those of a drunken man.

Since *prāṇa* is more abundant in woman, the master uses the breath to act upon her, and the rising of Kuṇḍalinī takes place easily; for while man emits, woman absorbs, she is able to assimilate great powers and may prove mightier than man. For what characterizes woman is the expansion of the central way: in her, the energy of the center in *suṣumnānāḍī* or in *madhyanāḍī*, as well as the womb, are in constant expansion.

At the end of the process, neither *vīrya* nor *prāṇa* remain, and instead there is a very pure essence, "*mahārasa*." As his *madhyacakra* is turned upward, the male stores this essence in the *brahmarandhra* and brings it down whenever he wants to use it. A *guru* treasures up this essence as the most precious thing, the best of all energies, never to be wasted and exclusively to be employed for spiritual purposes. Indeed, by means of this pure essence, he progresses by leaps and bounds in mystical life. Once he masters this power, which he holds in great respect, he no longer loses it, even if the body is old or exhausted.

The woman does not keep this pure essence in the *brahmarandhra*, but in *madhyagarbha* or in *suṣumnā* which unfolds; thence the essence spreads to *madhyacakra*, the central wheel, which in her is steady.

As for union between a master and his female disciple, it requires a master who is both qualified and perfect to bring down this pure substance thus kept in store and infuse it into woman. When a sanctified child is conceived, this transference occurs through sexual union; but it may take place without this agency, if master and disciple are united by a very pure love, a love which is free of all desire.*

* Notice. If "efficience", an archaic term meaning "the exercise of efficient power" (*The Shorter English Dictionary on Historical Principles*) has been used in the present translation, it is to avoid the technical connotations of "efficiency" and in the hope of suggesting more than "efficacy" does, though, of course, even a rare word cannot convey the exceptional significance of *vīrya* in those ancient texts.

Chapter Five

Kulayāga, Esoteric Sacrifice

Excerpts from *Tantrāloka*, Chapter XXIX

Definition

Abhinavagupta regards as of primary importance these *kula* practices, revealed to him by his master Śambunātha and of which he gives a lengthy account in *Tantrāloka*, chapter XXIX, under the denomination of *rahasyacarcāvidhi,* secret rite.

1. Now is described the secret rite designed for master and disciple who have reached the summit [of mystical life]; [resting in the *nirvikalpa* state, beyond all duality, they are free of attachment and limitation].

2–3. In the *Kramapūjātantra* the Lord has unveiled the essence thereof. That which is achieved in one single month by the method of the *siddha*—accomplished beings—cannot be obtained in a thousand years through the medium of ordinary ceremonies or of a flood of mantra . . .

4. *Kula* conveys the ideas of energy of the

Lord, efficience, elevation, freedom, vitality, virile potency, *piṇḍa,*[1] consciousness and body.

5. This sacrifice is meant only for one who thus sees everything in the same light, freed from all doubts.

6. Is called *kula* sacrifice whatever the hero (*vīra*) accomplishes in thought, word, or deed, through any activity [requiring boldness and heroism] apt to reveal such essence.

7. Notwithstanding this variety of conditions, the sacrifice may be performed in six different ways: in worldly activities, in relation to a woman [through a mere glance], in the couple's union, as well as in body, breath,[2] and thought.

8. It needs no sacrificial circle, fire-pit, ritual purifications, baths . . . , in short, none of the objects and instruments usually associated with rites.

9. According to the *Triśirobhairava*: " . . . it is nothing but knowledge and knowable."

10. Still, to the wise are prescribed practices which are forbidden in other religious treatises: [the use of meat, of alcoholic liquors, and sexual union (*maithunī*)].

The next verses describe the outer ritual and are of little interest as far as Kuṇḍalinī is concerned. Let us only mention the reverence for the lineage of masters (*nātha*) and for their energies (*yoginī*). The *mudrā* specific to each of them are listed, as well as the raised Kuṇḍalinī and secret seats such as the *dvādaśānta*, *bhrū*, the heart, the navel, and the bulb.

Which masters are qualified to perform this *yāga*? There are three types of *siddha*, distinguished by how they use their *vīrya*, this very pure essence that resides, unstirred, in the superior center.

Some are *ūrdhvareta*, chaste men who keep it permanently

1. *Piṇḍa,* a solid mass, a dense one-savored whole.
2. In *madhyanāḍī.*

in this center,[3] thus preserving their virility. Endowed with knowledge and not with potency, they have few disciples and are neither *kaula* masters nor *brahmacārin* suited for the *kaula* way.

To the contrary, when virility is stirred up in ordinary men and in the *kaula* adepts, it goes down to the so-called 'generation seat' (*janmasthāna*). And while the former are not aware of the process, the latter are fully conscious of it and have control over their *vīrya*; thus they are simultaneously endowed with knowledge and potency. Such *kaula* masters, votaries of *brahman* and of the three prohibitions, are qualified to initiate a great number of disciples.

Then, according to the *Kālīkulatantra*, another class of *siddha*, solely through their subtle bodies, penetrate, during their sports with *yoginī*, into the bodies of very pure men and women in order to arouse in them a mutual desire; it is from this union that is born the exceptional child known as *yoginībhū*.[4]

Next comes the description of the great ceremony: selected place, fragrant garlands, identification with Bhairava, contemplation of the master, ascent of Kuṇḍalinī in the median way, fire oblation, etc. Then the *dūtī* is brought along: she and her partner engage in mutual worship by identifying with Śakti and Śiva.

Vidhi of the *Dūtī* or *Ādiyāga*[5]

> 96. This secret ritual revealed by the Lord is now described. Let it be performed in the company of an outer energy [a woman called *dūtī*].

"Just as the *brahman*'s[6] wife takes part in the Vedic ritual, so does the *dūtī* participate in the *kulācārya* practice," says a verse.

> 97–98. According to the *Yogasaṃcāratantra*, the state of *brahmacārin* must be observed. *Brahman* is supreme bliss and resides in the

3. They are, according to *Maheśvarānanda* (M.M. śl. 39), initiate princes (*rājapūtra*).
4. *Śl.* 40–45. Cf. here p. 174.
5. T.A. XXIX, śl 96–168.
6. Who presides over Vedic ceremonies.

body in three ways: the first two are used as means, the third one, identical with bliss, is the fruit thereof.

The former include meat and alcohol; the third one is sexual union, through which one becomes aware of bliss. This is what is referred to as the three *M*s.

99–100. Enslaved beings who are deprived of the three *M*s [usually forbidden] are deprived of bliss altogether. Those who perform the sacrifice without the three *M*s, sources of bliss, also go to a dreadful hell.

Verse 99 and its gloss specify that only the heroic being[7] may resort to these means to achieve brahmic plenitude, for, in order to be a *brahmacārin*, one must indeed avail oneself of the three prohibited means, the supreme *brahman* being bliss and bliss being revealed in the body through them. Here one should be very careful: to enjoy or to dispense with those three *M*s may lead to unfortunate consequences; he who is not a hero and indulges in them without performing *kulayāga*, and he who, having performed the rite, refuses to further enjoy it, are equally in danger of falling into hell.

100–101. The sole distinctive feature of the energy—woman—is the faculty she has of identifying with the owner of the energy—man or *sādhaka*. Her selection, therefore, should be made irrespective of her beauty, caste, etc.

What sort of woman enables the *sādhaka* to realize his true nature?

Her beauty, caste or birth are immaterial, for a bold, virile (*vīra*) mind, free of doubt and wavering, is enough to qualify the *dūtī* for this sacrifice. And she must also have the same heart, the same intention as the *vīra*, in view of their identification during *samādhi*.

7. *Vīrasādhaka*.

101–102. Since such identity is beyond all worldly or supraworldly association [ties of blood or of the mind], this energy is given three different names in my master's tradition—cause, subsequent effect and simultaneous birth[8]—and again is threefold, directly or indirectly [that is, cause of the cause, effect of the effect, etc.].

Noteworthy is the choice of terms referring to these three types of partners; *hetu* is the "cause", and, though the term is glossed as *janikā* (that which brings forth), she is not the natural mother—just as *kārya* is not the daughter—but a divine *dūtī* who, infusing boldness and power into her partner, acts as an initiator to him.

Kārya, textually "that which has to be done" and is a response to an incentive or an effect, appears as a *dūtī* initiated by a master or a more advanced *sādhaka* who "induces" in her a state free of doubt and fear.

Sahotthā, "that which arises at the same time," acts as a spiritual sister (*sahajā*) toward a *sādhaka*. The potency (*vīratā*) which she enjoys spontaneously becomes manifest in both of them at the same time.

It is in this figurative sense that should be interpreted a number of tantric passages alluding to union with mother, daughter, or sister, a wording which brings about the reprobation of all those who stick to the letter.

Jayaratha quotes an unambiguous stanza in this connection: "Neither wife, sister, mother, daughter, nor intimate friend are allowed to take part in this ceremony."

If the wife is kept aside, this is because of attachment to her, as union has no other purpose than a heroic course of action.[9]

Another verse further removes all ambiguity: "For this sacrifice, let the *dūtī* be selected without any misleading by sexual desire."

Here union serves only to bring to the surface the latent abilities of the adept. This sacrifice is not performed with the enjoyment born of desire (*kāma*) in view, but in order to probe into one's own heart and ascertain the steadiness of one's own mind.

8. Here these terms refer to three levels of birth into spiritual life: anterior birth, posterior birth, and simultaneous birth.

9. Cf. M.M. *śl* 38, commentary pp. 133–135 but if there is no attachment union is licit.

103. As succintly asserted by the *Sarvācārahṛdaya*: "It is said that there are six energies bestowing fructification[10] and liberation."

One stanza gives the list of these six energies: "*Vegavatī*, stimulus or impulse aroused in the *sādhaka* during union. *Saṃhārī*, the energy of absorption, which takes one deep within. *Trailokyakṣobhanī*, the energy that brings excitation to a climax, as related to the triad. *Ardhavīrāsanā*, the energy through which one is firmly established in sexual intercourse. *Vaktrakaula*, the orgasm at the end of the process. The sixth energy is the woman, *dūtī*.[11]

All these energies assist the *sādhaka* during the ceremony, so that he becomes deeply absorbed in the internal organ hereafter described:

104. Emission and resorption are engendered by both [partners], for the best of rites is the union [of Śiva and Śakti].

How is it performed? Through physical union:

105. When the *dūtī* is present, both of them engage in mutual worship, finding satisfaction in the intimate organ [the heart]; they pay homage to the main wheel. The intimate organ of consciousness is the one wherefrom bliss flows out.[12]

The gloss further states that the intimate part or organ refers either to the heart or to the sexual organs, according to whether the rite is purely interior or completely exterior. Both aspects develop in fact simultaneously: the inner sacrifice concerns the main wheel, the outer sacrifice, the secondary wheels corresponding to the sense organs.

Main Wheel and Secondary Wheels

106–107. Such is the main wheel; the sec-

10. The fruit and enjoyment in this world, the complement of liberation.
11. Within whom he loses himself.
12. Although suffused with the joy of love, here bliss is not that of ordinary desire.

ondary wheels are inferior to it. The term *cakra* [wheel] is associated with some verbal roots meaning: to expand [the essence] (*kaś*); to be satisfied [in this essence] (*cak*-); to break the bonds (*kṛt*-) and to act efficiently (*kṛ*-). So the wheel expands, is satisfied, breaks, and has the power to act.[13]

This etymology, in Indian fashion, accounts for the transferring from *anucakra* to *madhyacakra*, and thence to Śiva.

That which generates bliss and that which enraptures the heart indeed befit such worship.

How should the main wheel be honored? Through the outer sacrifice, which satiates and expands consciousness:

107. And again, externally, the sacrifice is a satisfaction hailed as a blooming out.

Satisfaction leads to the cessation of desire, and the blooming out of consciousness appears as a great fervor.[14]

108–109. The vibrant fervor of consciousness may be due to outer substances, flowers, perfumes and incense which act upon the breath; also to food, wherefrom pleasure is derived. This fervor again is aroused when the owner of the energy (*sādhaka*) imagines the kisses, etc., and so penetrates into the main wheel and the secondary wheels.

109–110. This is how [the *sádhaka* and his partner] should, with the help of suitable substances, mutually satiate their secondary wheels so that these become one with the main wheel.

13. We shall see what is meant by unfoldment and satisfaction of consciousness. The broken bonds are those of sex, when man and woman, during union, are oblivious of all duality.

14. *Ucchalana.*

Through all these sensations corresponding to their secondary centers, colors for the eyes, sounds for the ears, kisses for the touch . . . the satisfaction is such that the secondary centers are drawn back to the main Center and identify with the wheel of Consciousness.

According to these verses, one should be satiated so that intense fervor may surge. *Ucchalana* therefore plays a fundamental part, first as vibration (*spanda*)—the prefix *ut-* denotes a rising, and *chal-* an effervescence, a clash—hence the intensely vibrant ascent of Kuṇḍalinī, the sexual center becoming the chief instrument to this vibrant and conscious unification, which has the heart for its support.

Henceforth are met all the prerequisites to the *kramamudrā*, an attitude which is so difficult to attain and through which interior and exterior worlds are equalized.

In a treatise where Śiva is questioned by the Goddess, the *caryākrama* is favorably substituted for the elements of the Vedic rite:

> "What is it that should be worshipped? Women are worshipped.
>
> Who is the worshipper? Man is the worshipper.
>
> Who invokes the deity? Their mutual love.
>
> Which flower is offered? The scratches made by the nails.
>
> What are the incense and the oblation? Embrace and caresses.
>
> What is the mantra? The beloved's flow of words.
>
> What is the recitation? The pleasure of the lips.
>
> What is the sacrificial pit? The womb.
>
> What is the wood [of the sacrificial ladle]? The *liṅga*.
>
> What is the fire? The sprout in the womb.
>
> What is the clarified butter? The seed (*bīja*) or *vīrya* (sperm), according to the *Bhairavāgama*.
>
> What is, O Master of the Gods, the *samā-*

dhi? And Śiva answers: Sound, touch, form, savor and odor, just as the flow of bliss is released, what issues from these sensations in a fivefold way, that is *samādhi*. Having realized this, let one obtain Śiva."

110–111. This is what is stated in the *Triśirastantra*: "He whose abode is the very pure absorption [of union] in the midst of the six sense activities, will penetrate to the seat of Rudra."[15]

During sexual union, although the yogin sees and feels, and all his organs are at the height of their power, still he never ceases keeping absorbed and he remains aware of his being pure Knower. All the tendencies of the secondary centers rush toward the main wheel when this *saṃpuṭīkaraṇa* takes place for the first time, while the yogin is immersed in the Self.[16]

111–112. In the intense realization of his own essence, which fully blooms out with the extension of varied enjoyments [colors, sounds, etc.] related to their respective secondary wheels, the divine energies find access one after the other to the central wheel of Consciousness.

Then flashes the wonder of Self-discovery, since the central wheel is the resting place of universal Consciousness, the Reality of the supreme Subject and its highest bliss.

But, it may be objected, is it not the same with anyone engaging in ordinary union? Of what avail is such a union in mystical life?

112–113. For the other beings attached to their own ego and who, on account of their prejudices concerning "I" and "you", are deprived of such a realization, the energies of their secondary

15. About *rudrayāmala*, cf. here p. 137.

16. This process which contracts all the organs together occurs a second time during the immersion in Paramaśiva, cf. here pp. 169.

wheels remain distinct; they are neither vibrating nor endowed with plenitude.

As the unfolding of consciousness is essential for such a sacrifice, not everyone is entitled to it. Ordinary man cannot reach fulfillment thereby: as his desires have not disappeared, for him union does not lead to Self-consciousness. As such, it is useless and even blameworthy from the spiritual and mundane points of view. Thus, two kinds of sexual union are to be distinguished: a worldly one, leading to the inferior domain (*adhodhāman*), and a mystical one, leading to the superior domain (*ūrdhvadhāman*), for, Kuṇḍalinī being awakened, the agitation of the couple passes from the secondary centers to the main Center, since *anucakra* and *madhyacakra* are no longer apart.

113–114. Ardently turning to each other, the couple formed by the energy and the owner thereof, filled with the rays radiating from the energies of the secondary wheels, thus obtains efficience.

All the organs of man and woman are, at this stage, permeated with power (*vīrya*).

Description of *Madhyacakra* or *Ūrdhvadhāman*

114–115. When the couple penetrates into the superior domain, there occurs an intense agitation (*saṃkṣobha*) owing to this contact; then even the secondary wheels are stirred and identify with this domain [of consciousness] from which they are no longer separate.

A feeling of plenitude arises in the yogin who loses the sense of identification with his body. Such is the agitation induced by vibration (*spanda*). Once man and woman thus stirred reach the main center, their secondary centers participate in this agitation owing to their being united to the superior center.

A second *sampuṭīkaraṇa* follows after the first one. While the agitation of the organs at first enables the penetration into the center where they unite and identify, the center afterward expands, vibrates, and the agitation is then transmitted from the center to the fully awakened organs. The couple reaches the great bliss center known as "mouth of the *yoginī*"[17] and, in the effervescence of union, the enraptured discovery of the Self displaces the perception of the body.

Śāntodita. Quiescent and Emergent

> 115–116. Thus this union, wherein all differentiated knowledge gradually fades away as penetration into the central wheel progresses, is Consciousness itself, the unitive friction of the two flows of emission.[18] Such is the highest, permanent and most noble abode, universal bliss having the two as its essence.[19] It is neither quiescence nor emergence, but their original cause; this is the supreme secret of *kula*.

The union ends with the internal emission, an emission which never occurs in ordinary union and leads to the *kramamudrā*. The practice must be simultaneously performed by man and woman, for its purpose is generating universal bliss rather than pleasure; moreover, it enables one to gain access to *samādhi* effortlessly, even during the ordinary state.[20]

The commentator points out that at the time of the supreme union of a mystical order, as consciousness becomes revealed, universal bliss is then suffused with the unique savor[21] of Śiva and Śakti now one. Quiescence or rest within one's own essence is thus transcendent with regard to the world, whereas emergence is

17. Or *mukhavaktra*, chief mouth equivalent to the center.

18. *Visarga*, emission, flow of *vīrya*, efficience, sperm or external flow, then internal flow made of pure spiritual efficience.

19. Śiva and Śakti on the cosmic plane, man and woman on the human plane.

20. *Vyutthāna*.

21. *Sāmarasya*.

immanent in it. Reality is *kaula*, true Consciousness, boundless, the source of the quiescent state and of the emergent state, although being neither.

Kula is the mystery beyond the quiescent and emergent states. The external flow (*udita*) and the internal flow (*śānta*) function by turn, and each only for a moment. In this way the unitive friction of the two flows of emission occurs.

Fruit of This Activity

> 117. This Consciousness [identical with his own essence], he who wishes to reach this infinite domain must make it his own again and again, because the nature of divine Consciousness, from the standpoint of the absolute, is boundless.

How does one enter this infinite domain?

> 118–119. Let the blissful one penetrate into the boundless domain,[22] [in the center] of the [internal] emission, by watching how the quiescent and emergent modalities referred to as "this" and "that" arise and subside.

This domain is beyond expression, for it is experienced only for oneself when the external function ceases, and at the beginning of the internal *visarga*; as all differentiation has vanished, the couple becomes immersed in the flow of the interior domain—a center free from all the limitations of "this" and "that," namely of such and such a quality; the means of penetration into the center must disappear, as indicated in the *Vijñānabhairava* (*śl.* 62):

> "After it has left one object aside, let not the

22. Here *dhāman* assumes its many meanings: divine abode, energy, brightness, splendor, majesty; it is the *anavacchinnapada* and universal bliss (*jagadānanda*).

mind move toward any other; then, in and through the middle, the Realization will entirely unfold in all its intensity."

What are man's and woman's reciprocal parts on entering the infinite domain?

119–120. These quiescent and emergent aspects then arise simultaneously in the energy and in the owner thereof. If both reach this domain at the same time and by way of reciprocity, this is emergence; but if they reach it only within themselves, this is the quiescent aspect. Nonetheless both actually form a couple in quiescence as well as in emergence.

If, during the *śānta* stage, *yoginī* and *siddha* enjoy peace similarly but each for himself, this rest, however does not take place independently of their union, for the appeasement corresponds to their simultaneously obtaining a *samādhi* with Self-awakening induced by a unifying dive into the main and intimate center. The emergent state concerns man and woman ardently turned toward each other; since *samādhi* then spreads in *vyutthāna* (in wakefulness and in sleep), the energy becomes divinized in its varied aspects.

Differences between Man's and Woman's Parts During Identification.

121. Although both are equally possessed of the awareness of the quiescent and emergent states, the energy alone, and not the owner, is capable of developing creation . . .

She alone has the capacity of bearing and nourishing the embryo and of making the emission fruitful.

122–123. On the subject of woman, treatises

state that her median way[23] fully expands. And so to her alone should the *guru* impart the whole of the secret doctrine (*kulārtha*); and through her, by the practice of union . . . it is imparted to men.

Appeased in man, the *suṣumnānāḍī* is full-blown in woman. A great master, therefore, is in possession of this function through an initiated woman. Śivānandanātha, the founder of the Krama school, did not impart his doctrine to a disciple but to three *yoginī* who, in their turn, initiated some men.

The commentary quotes a verse: "What is achieved by a *sādhaka* after engaging in this practice for a whole year, a woman obtains in a single day."

124. In short, the venerable Kallaṭanātha has stated about woman that, as regards the body, she is endowed with a pure, eminent substance.

124–125. The Lord calls this central wheel "mouth of the *yoginī*," for thereupon is based the transmission of the spiritual lineage[24] and therefrom is Knowledge obtained. This Knowledge beyond duality cannot be described and it is rightly said to be transmitted from mouth to mouth.

126. And the mouth is the main wheel. How could we possibly account for our own consciousness?

Knowledge implies an absorption in the supreme Consciousness.

A distinction should be drawn between the inferior mouth—the aperture of the organs—and the chief mouth,[25] identical with Consciousness, the only one to be a divine womb.[26] The latter should therefore be full of consciousness. How could we possibly depict such things which are a matter of experience? One cannot

23. *Madhyamapada* or *suṣumnānāḍī*.
24. *Sampradāya*.
25. *Upavaktra* and *madhyavaktra* or *yoginīvaktra* respectively.
26. *Yoni*.

indeed go further back than Consciousness, the principle of universal explanation.

> 126–127. They gain access to the boundless domain those who, during this double emission—the quiescent and emergent domains—mightily grasp the reality of the emission preceding them.

This is *parakaula*, the source of emission. Those beings who have but one longing, liberation, are fully aware that here everything is but the unfoldment of the real *visarga* or of the union of its poles.

Twice, but on different planes, do the same states manifest, emergence at the beginning of union and quiescence at the end.

To obtain *siddhi*, one is advised to concentrate on the emergent rather than on the quiescent phase, in order to avoid the appeased self-absorption, which does not grant any power.

> 128–129. Those wishing to acquire efficience must feed upon the emergent form. Through it, let them worship [the wheel of energies] for, on account of its being close to Consciousness, this emergent form is extremely pure; it goes from the chief mouth [that of the *yoginī*] to [the adept's] own mouth and vice versa. Bestower of immortality and youth, it is named *kula*, supreme.

This mouth is "a ewer presented to the guest. It is through its wonderful savor that all the gods are worshipped." And another verse reads thus: "Having performed this sacrifice by the mouth-to-mouth process, let one worship the Wheel associated with the efficience of the organs, that noble essence (*mahārasya*). In this way is Śiva ever worshipped and death conquered."

This exchange from one mouth to another alludes to a customary practice in Kashmirian marriage: the couple stands inside a circle and the bridegroom's mother puts in her son's mouth a morsel of food which he cuts into two; one piece he introduces into the bride's mouth and she in her turn puts a morsel in the mouth of the bridegroom. However, in the esoteric practice, woman is the repository of the pure substance transferred to man and returning to her during an unceasing interchange.

The process of breath and efficience going from the *yoginī*'s mouth to the *siddha* and vice-versa is precisely *saṃputīkaraṇa*, a prefiguration of *kramamudrā*. *Prāṇa* and *vīrya* are so intimately mixed as to be transformed into each other and to become one and the same. According to the tradition, the adept is rejuvenated; white hair and wrinkles disappear. At this stage, the couple has gained mastery over *vīrya*.

The practice heretofore described, concerning one endowed with Knowledge (*jñānin*), goes without regulations. But those who are devoid of Knowledge and engage in *caryākrama* must follow the prescribed rules, progressing step by step in accordance with the *kramapūjā*: worship, union (*udita*), then appeasement (*śānta*). First they worship outside, in the energy circle, then within their own bodies according to the worship described in chapter XV of the *Tantrāloka*.

129–132. As for those who have not reached full discrimination, they too will obtain Knowledge (*vijñāna*) by taking part in the sacrifice which attains completion in the state of emergence,[27] after they have worshipped the divine energies of the main wheel evoked during this sacrifice. And there, in the wheel of energy, they worship these divinities in accordance with the method mentioned, with the help [of the emergent form] full of the very savor of bliss, starting from the outside: Ganeśa, with his attendants in the four spatial directions, the couple of the Kula masters [Śiva and the energy] in the center; the three goddesses[28] at the three points of the trident and, externally, four goddesses at each point. Let the *muni* also worship a twelve-spoked wheel or one octad, or else eight octads . . .

133. Let the worship of those same divinities

27. That of sexual union.

28. The three goddesses are the supreme, intermediate, and non-supreme energies.

be performed not only in the wheel of energy, but also in the domain of one's own body.

Knowledge is obtained during unbroken concentration upon the flow corresponding to the emergent form of union.

The Triple *Visarga*: Quiescence, Emergence, and *Kaula*

133–135. If, with the consciousness of the Heart thus exercised by means of any practice whatsoever, the quiescent form of Śiva manifests, one then gains access to the appeased state, similar to an unruffled sea.[29]

When one becomes established in that state, the whole host of the divine energies of the [main] wheel stands still, free of fluctuation, suspended in the void, in undivided beatitude.

According to one verse the void corresponds to the supreme, unrelated Śiva. Complete bliss (*nirānanda*) accrues from repose in Śiva. The central wheel concerns only touch; as to the secondary or minor wheels, with their qualities of sound, form, odor, and taste, the author further states:

135–136. [The energies] of the secondary wheels—sight, hearing—also participate in this essence, for they depend on the energies of the main wheel; immersed in bliss, they remain immobile, yearning for bliss.

Objection: If the energies of the minor centers become appeased in the very midst of bliss, why is it said that they long for bliss?

136–137. Having no contact with the supreme essence, all the energies of the sense or-

29. From *śāntarūpābhyāsa* arises *śāntaśivapada*.

> gans remain immobile, deprived of their own essences and craving for them.[30]

At first, owing to the peace that penetrates them, the sense organs gradually dissolve in the central wheel where they rest in the midst of the essence—the Consciousness of the supreme Subject—in a dense mass of bliss (*nirānanda*), without enjoying their respective pleasures, such as colors, sounds, tastes and smells. Here two conditions are required: firstly, the central wheel cannot be realized until the energies of the minor wheels gather in the center—which sexual union helps to bring about. Secondly, these wheels cannot be activated as long as the central wheel is not activated.

When the organs, henceforth saturated with their own essence, again long for the enjoyment of external things, even if they derive some pleasure from them for a split second, they at once offer this pleasure to the Self. All the sense energies begin to seek whatever they find worthy of being offered to their own nature in order to satiate the central wheel. They are compared to the buzzing bee that gathers honey from flower to flower for the sole benefit of the bee-hive.

> 137–139. [The whole of them], eager[31] to enjoy the sap of external things overflowing with their own savor and having obtained such or such appeased state owing to this satisfaction, are poured out as an offering into the Self.
>
> Through this offering of their respective objects—smells, sounds, tastes, shapes, touches —there gushes a stream which causes Consciousness to overflow and . . . reach at once a vibrant fervor,[32] the intense agitation of virile potency being due to this plenitude. And, as already

30. On this topic, refer to *Hymnes de Abhinavagupta*, pp. 87–90. In one of those hymns, the goddesses of the organs turn eagerly to the heart wherein dwells Bhairava.

31. *Raṇaraṇakara*, the cry of the torment of love and the onomatopoeia for the humming of the bee.

32. *Ucchal-*, on the inner *spanda*, extraordinary vibration associated with the ascent of Kuṇḍalinī, cf. here p. 76.

> said, the Lord of the wheel also expands impetuously.

The overflowing of the secondary energies thus gathered together brings to a climax the intensity of consciousness, namely that of the main wheel. At this moment the master of the conscious energies, the supreme Knower, makes a sudden rush toward the outer world.[33]

After describing emergence, Abhinavagupta treats the fusion of the two poles of emission:

Union or Fusion

> 140–142. Consequently, threefold is the flow (*visarga*): unitive, emergent and quiescent. If it is named "*sarga*,"[34] this is because from it flows the varied creation[35] and into it the creation returns; the *Tattvarakṣaṇa*, the *Triśiromata* and the *Nigamatantra* declare: "The pit is the energy, the *liṅga* is Śiva, and [their] union the supreme realm. From these two, creation and resorption respectively proceed."
>
> Such, according to the *Gamaśāstra*, is the triple flow.

The commentary posits the following correspondences:

Śakti = *udita* = *kuṇḍa* = *sṛṣṭi* (energy; emergence; pit; creative mode).

Śiva = *śānta* = *liṅga* = *saṃhāra* (Śiva; quiescence; *liṅga*; resorptive mode).

Melaka or *saṃghaṭṭa* = (fusion of Śiva and Śakti, supreme domain.)

> 142–143. [After bestowing] awakening, rest,

33. Jayaratha, in order to shed some light on these stanzas, quotes here verses 111–113.

34. *Vi-sarga,* i.e. *sarga,* flow and *vi-(citra),* varied.

35. The flow of *vīrya* and the rising of Kuṇḍalinī.

and absorption on the twin ascending and descending current up to its culmination in the central channel, after granting these likewise to the channels, the motions of the wheels, the junctions and joints, Śiva,[36] who for ever dwells in the Body endowed with 72,000 channels, brings each consciousness freed[37] from its ceaseless back and forth movement to fuse with the other.

144. Let one be eager to become ever more firmly established in this fusion, the bhairavian domain.

Śiva (or the mystic having identified with him) pacifies the breaths, awakens the centers, infuses the breaths into *madhyanāḍī*, mixing them in an undifferentiated union. Then he must develop a fervent yearning for the very essence of emergence and quiescence, that is, for their fusion into full consciousness, where they lose themselves.

145. That is for both what clearly reveals this "thing" free from parts and divisions, and characterized by the full attainment of modeless Reality.

Here all functions come to an end. The distinction between man and woman disappears; only union remains, wherein Śiva and Śakti, quiescence and emergence, become undistinguishable. "*Artha*," one single, indefinite form, is called a "thing" because it is grasped in an intimate and therefore inexpressible experience.

146–147. Let one thus turn away from the [various] modes by extracting sun and moon from the two ways of immersion and dispersion,

36. At that time the yogin experiences the seventy-two thousand *nāḍī* which, issuing from the *sahasrāra,* spread throughout his body.

37. *Antarā* is one of the many difficulties of these stanzas; must it be translated as "except" or "without," as construed by Jayaratha, or as "within"? In this context indeed, "without back and forth movement" or "within the back and forth movement" amounts much to the same idea.

and give oneself over to the Consciousness of [bhairavian] Reality.[38]

Cultivating the contact with Reality, that of the supreme Subject who, inside the median domain, is permeated by all things, one must maintain in the middle conduit the ascending and descending breaths emanated from the left and right channels, wherein they should neither dissolve nor disperse.

So that the nature of this Reality (*bhāva*) may be better apprehended, Abhinavagupta describes it from different angles, defining it in relation to *dhvani, japa,* and *mudrā*. *Dhvani* is a spontaneous sound vibration, similar to that issuing from the Beloved's lips.[39] *Japa* is *nāda*, an ever-surging resonance; it is practised by unifying the secondary centers inside the main center.

Mantravīrya Peculiar to *Dhvani*, Sound Vibration

147–148. Thus the sound vibration, which is perfect Self-awareness, arises in the domain of union during absorption in the consciousness of the triple flow. Such is the power of the *mantra*.

The efficience is that of the mantra "*aham*", the supreme "I". The vibrant resonance (*dhvani*) becomes manifest once the three flows spontaneously coincide (*samāpatti*) in perfect union.

148–149. He alone truly knows the emergence of the mantra who, in this very resonance, with a wish to obtain such fruits of emergence, remains absorbed in his own mantra.

The moment he finds himself in the very midst of the vibrant, wonder-struck awareness, that of *dhvani*, the *sādhaka* must unite

38. Here there is a play on the word *bhāva*, meaning both spontaneous Reality grasped through the heart during bhairavian union (*kaula*), and differentiated realities. Since Jayaratha does not give any explanation, this stanza may be translated in different ways.

39. Cf. here p. 152.

the mantra received from his master with the inner resonance and through his vigilance he will come to understand what the performance of the mantra truly means.

> 149–150. It is there again—in full awareness—just as the secondary wheels rush all at once [into the central wheel] of Consciousness and identify with it, that, with the help of sound, he should simultaneously perform *japa* in the form of different *lakṣa*.

To shed some light on this stanza, Jayaratha quotes two verses (p. 104): according to one, the energies gain access, one after another, to the central wheel of Consciousness; the other further states that *japa* recitation consists of three *lakṣa* (100,000 recitations): one in the emergence (of the minor wheels), a second in quiescence (when those wheels converge in consciousness), and a third in the fusion (their identification) within the central wheel.

Any power thus acquired by 300,000 recitations (*japa*) is gained in a single moment through the simultaneity of emergence, quiescence and fusion.

The Supreme Mystical Attitude. *Khecarīmudrā*

> 150–151. As stated in the *Yogasaṃcāra*, such a union is the supreme attitude, cherished by the *yoginī*. A [three-petalled] lotus sits hidden in an ever-unfolding circle resting inside a triangle.
>
> [In the middle] of this lotus and inseparable from it, resides a stem whose strong root is adorned with a sixteen-petalled[40] lotus flower.
>
> 152–153. The shoot is emitted [on three conditions]: 1. Owing to the successive frictions of the two lotuses strung on the stem standing upright in the center. 2. Owing to the union of ovum

40. The sixteen *kalā* or lunar portions.

> and sperm[41] in the three-petalled lotus. 3. Owing to the unitive friction in fire (the Subject) of the energy waves of the fully resplendent rays of the sun and the moon. And this shoot is creation itself.

The three-petalled lotus stands for the ever-expanding womb. Sexual bliss makes manifest the stem or median channel, the domain wherefrom arises the root of creative emission. On this stem two triangles represent man and woman ardently turned toward each other, that is, Śiva and Śakti in perfect union. These triangles having a common center are interconnected by one single thread, the median way. The friction of those two triangles arouses Kuṇḍalinī, and when her ascent is completed, the triangles meet and fuse into a six-pointed figure, the Seal of Solomon.

In fire—the Knower—takes place the fusion of the gloriously-shining rays of both sun and moon, namely: knowledge and known, expired and inspired breaths, sperm and blood (*rakta*), all those rays that radiate bliss.

A verse further states:

> "When knowledge and known unite, the knower appears."

Agni, fire or subject, becomes manifest in a twofold way: at the general level, as supporting the seed of the universe which it raises up to the Fourth state, and, at the individual level, as sustaining the embryo in the three-petalled lotus—the womb—by means of a flow of semen and blood.

So from the shoot proceeds the emission, that of the ascending Kuṇḍalinī and that wherefrom the child will be born.

When ovum and sperm unite, the three main centers[42] become one: the mouth of the *yoginī* identifies with the heart, and the *brahmarandhra* fills the womb or *yoginīvaktra*. Henceforth no other place remains than the universal median domain, beyond male and female bodies, beyond the centers. This practice is called *yoginībhū*, for such a womb expands ad infinitum[43] by virtue of the all-pervasiveness of the mantra.

41. *Rajas* and *aruṇa* in woman, *vīrya* and *retas* in man.
42. That is, *yoginīvaktra, hṛdaya,* and *brahmarandhra.*
43. *Yoginīvikāsa.*

Effect of this Mystical Attitude

> 153–154. He suddenly becomes rooted in the Fourth state who, by means of this *mudrā* wherein moon, sun and fire coalesce, internally takes hold of the processes of emission, resorption. . .

He is indeed as if "sealed" (*mud-*); such a *mudrā* is called '*khecarī*', "which roams in the ether of ultimate Consciousness (*kha*)" and which, associated with Śiva and the energy, assumes the form of the eightfold wheel.

> 154–155. The power of the mantra consists in an awareness which flashes in the energy and the owner when, penetrating into this *khecarīmudrā*, they embrace, rejoice, laugh and play the game of love.
>
> 156. This awareness manifests through the eight stages of Sound: non-manifested, sound-vibration and humming sound [in sexual union or *udita*], outburst of sound, murmur, resonance and end of the resonance [revealing themselves successively in the quiescence of *śānta*]. As to the unuttered and unbroken sound, it is related to union.[44]

Kisses and other manifestations pertaining to the secondary centers make it easier to enter the central wheel, this penetration being precisely the *khecarīmudrā*. How could one give an idea of this fundamental experience? The various enjoyments are part of it, but similar to weightless clouds drifting in the infinite sky, hence

44. Respectively: *avyakta, dhvani, rāva, sphoṭa, śruti, nāda, nādānta* and *anāhata*. There can be only an approximate rendering for those terms, for our language lacks proper words to denote those subtle sounds of a mystical order, which our civilization has neither experienced nor known about. Cf. table p. 205.

an all-encompassing and all-magnifying liberty, Ultimate Consciousness and the fully-active manifested energy being one.

> 156–157. He who gains access to the eightfold wheel utters the spontaneous *japa* inside the supreme domain and achieves the state of the eight *bhairava*, itself dividing into eight energies.

Once he penetrates into the eightfold wheel, he recognizes the eight *bhairava* or conscious subjects, the rulers of sounds whose eight *kalā*[45] extend from the half-moon to the energy beyond all thought.

> 157–158. [This octuple wheel[46] unfolds], during union, in the back and forth movement [of the inspired and expired breaths], in the certainty [peculiar to the intellect], in hearing, sight, the initial contact of both organs, in sexual union and at the extremity of the body [superior center or *dvādaśānta*] and finally in the wheel of union (*yāmalacakra*) [formed by all this].
>
> 158–159. There is an undefined[47] sound arising from the heart and which, moving through the bosom [of the beloved], reaches the throat and ends up on the lips. He who, just as agitation subsides, hears it at the center of both wheels [Śiva and Śakti], enjoys the ultimate appeasement (*nirvāṇa*).
>
> 159–160. The supreme Bhairava residing there as supreme Sound, endowed with eight aspects, made of light, of sound vibrations and of touch, is known as the very eminent omnipenetration [of the mantra *aham*, the absolute "I"].

Mantravyāpti, owing to its endless extension and deepening, is aptly called "very eminent." The spontaneously arising sound is

45. Cf. here p. 49, the sound-energies of the *praṇava OṂ*.
46. The wheel of union.
47. About *śītkāra*, cf. here p. 152.

fully appeased. The supreme resonance of Bhairava, identical with this complete pervasion,[48] consists of becoming aware of the inner wheel or *yoginīvaktra* when sexual agitation comes to an end; the light corresponds to the half-moon, the sound-vibration (*dhvani*) to the resonance (*nāda*), and touch to energy (*śakti*).

Definition of Omnipenetration (*Mantravyāpti*)

> 160–161. The eight *bhairava*[49] are given the following names: Related to a Certain Meaning,[50] Lord of the Undivided,[51] Void,[52] Pregnant with Meaning, Adorned with Etheric Void, Destroyer, the One Standing Within, and Guttural-labial. Such is the omnipenetration extending from the half-moon to *unmanā*.
>
> 161–163. He who, in his every act [of union] remains heedful of this pervasion, ever undefiled, is one liberated-in-life, and he identifies with the supreme Bhairava. The extraordinary being whose body is begotten in the womb during such a union is known as a "*yoginī*'s son"; he is Rudra, the worthy recipient of the spontaneous mystical Knowledge. Of him the *Vīrāvaliśāstra* says that while still an infant in the maternal womb, he is truly Śiva himself, [this, however, cannot be clearly expounded].
>
> 164–166. This sacrifice is termed "original" or primordial (*ādiyāga*) because through it the essence is grasped (*ādā*), and because it is the

48. *Nādabhairava* or *paramantravyāpti*.

49. Jayaratha does not give any elucidation about these aspects of the subjects characterized as *bhairava*. The corresponding energies extend from *ardhacandra* to *unmanā*. Cf. table p. 205.

50. *Sakala*, "endowed with parts", the initial stage of union, that is, a differentiated contact with the sense organs.

51. *Niṣkala*, "undivided," refers to that which has no contact with them.

52. The Void, *śūnya*, is more deeply appeased than the two former *bhairava*.

original sacrifice (*ādi*). It has been extolled by the Lord in the *Vīrāvalitantra*, the *Hṛdayabhaṭṭāraka*, the *Khecarīmata,* and other *tantra*.

Rahasyopaniṣad Krama

In this "process of the mystical and secret doctrine," the body is regarded as the supreme wheel.

166–168. By means of the couple of man and woman and without resorting to vows, to yoga . . . the *guru*, ever evoking the original sacrifice, engages therein, and lays on the female body and on his own body, science and efficience respectively. He meditates on the lotus [woman] in the form of the moon [knowable], and on himself in the form of the sun [knowledge]. Then he intimately merges together these two sanctuaries made up of Science (*vidyā*) and efficience (*mantra*).

169. Since this doctrine is a deep secret, I am not delineating it clearly. He who is interested therein may read the treatises.

171–173. The body itself is the supreme wheel, the eminent, beneficent *liṅga*, the chosen [place] of the divinized energies[53] and the realm of the highest worship (*pūjā*). It is indeed the chief *maṇḍala* composed of the triple trident, the lotuses, the centers, and the etheric void (*kha*).

There, all the [divinized] energies are ceaselessly worshipped, both externally and internally. Then, in full awareness of the *mantra*, let them, through a process of emission and resorption, be put in contact with the blissful and

53. Textually, the wheel of the divinities.

manifold sap issuing from the main wheel of energies.

174–175. Through this contact, the wheel of consciousness suddenly awakens and he who has sovereignty over it reaches the supreme domain, where all his bodily energies become satiated... Let him satisfy them externally by means of substances apt to unfold his heart, and internally through appropriate awakenings.

Then the master offers a prayer to the divine energy, Kuṇḍalinī, whom he worships as the support of birth; and by way of purification he presses the triple universe—knower, knowledge, and known—so as to extract its innumerable savors; the eminent nectar produced thereby, destroyer of birth, old age and death, is used as sacrificial butter fit to satisfy the supreme Goddess.

Here is the prayer that exemplifies the spirit of the *kula* practices and which Abhinavagupta cites on several occasions:

176–177. O vision of immortal and supreme ambrosia, resplendent with conscious light streaming from the absolute Reality, be my refuge. Through it art thou worshipped by those who know the mystical arcanum (*rahasya*).

Having purified the root support [the coiled-up Kuṇḍalinī] which I sprinkled with the savor of the wonder-struck Self-consciousness, and by offering the spiritual flowers of my own essence exhaling an innate scent, I worship Thee night and day, God united to the Goddess, in the divine sanctuary of my heart overflowing with ambrosial bliss.[54]

After the description of the ritual, Abhinavagupta concludes:

186–187. The master may thus initiate disciples, but only one out of one hundred thousand is worthy of such an initiation.

54. T.A. XXVI 63–64, X.350.

THE EIGHTFOLD WHEEL

The Rising of Kuṇḍalinī to *Unmanā* During Union

Couple	*NĀDA*, sounds	*KALĀ*, energies	ASPECTS of *NĀDA*	
United: *udita*	*avyakta*	*ardhacandra*	*jyotir (siddha)*	light
	dhvani	*nirodhikā*	*jyotir (yoginī)*	
	rāva	*nāda*	*dhvani (siddha)*	resonance
separated *śānta*	*sphoṭa*	*nādānta*	*dhvani (yoginī)*	
	śruti	*śakti*	*sparśa (siddha)*	touch
	nāda and *nādānta*	*vyāpinī*	*sparśa (yoginī)*	
fusion: *saṃghaṭṭa*	*anāhata*	*samanā*	fruit for	
		unmanā	the couple	

THE EIGHT BHAIRAVA[1]

Incarnations of the mantra

sakala, in contact with the organs	with respect to the *yoginī*	*adhacandra*
akala, without contact		*nirodhikā*
śūnya, void		*nāda*
kalādhya, rich in *kalā*	with respect to the *siddha*	*nādānta*
khamala vikṛta, adorned with *kha*		*śakti*
kṣepaṇaka, destroyer		*vyāpinī*
antaḥstha, standing within	with respect to the united couple	*samanā*
kaṇṭhyoṣṭhya, guttural-labial		*unmanā*

1. The classification of the eight *bhairava* differs somewhat from the former one.

CONCLUSION

Even when seen together, these texts, as said in the introduction, retain their mystery; they elude systematic or exhaustive exposition precisely because they are too rich in immediate experience, too careful as well to keep it concealed under the guise of revelation. This ever-present double aspect of mystery and revelation (*mahāguhya*) gives the reader the fascinating impression of a treasure which recedes the moment he is about to grasp it.

Yet the manifold aspects outlined here and the wide range of images conveying them help one to understand how the privileged experience of the yogin unfolds all the dimensions of life from the starting-point of ordinary consciousness, which the Kuṇḍalinī energy tears away from duality, unifies, universalizes and transfigures. Such indeed is the distinctive feature of the Kuṇḍalinī experience: to bring together the scattered elements of ordinary consciousness and merge them in the oneness of the original vibration and in the simultaneity of the differentiated levels. This it acheives without rupture or hiatus by simply bringing on the unfurling of all the successive planes, until the conscious energy moves freely from level to level, without imbalance or duality. This unfurling is neither imaginary nor speculative, even though poetic language and the arcane power of symbols are called upon for its expression.

With the ascent of Kuṇḍalinī, one detects, as it were, the mysterious upstream course thanks to which worldly energy turns into all-pervading consciousness. The stages of this transformation, wrought in the very body, thought, and word, depend on the interiorizing and unifying power of the Kuṇḍalinī energy, that is referred to any time a duality is resolved or the energy and Śiva become fused. On whatever level it was reigning supreme, duality dissolves into a oneness which breeds plenitude and initiates the development of the next stage. Thus complete oneness is achieved as intensity grows from *bindu* to *bindu*, until all of them merge into a single one, from bottom to top.

The unifying function of Kuṇḍalinī, when considered as it progresses from stage to stage, further reveals her power of pervasion, for she does not eradicate any plane or aspect but interiorizes them one by one, so as to permeate them with pure consciousness, once the latter has been reached.

Thus she operates in the great life centers that are the ingoing and outgoing breaths, the heart throb, the vibration of sound utterance and sexual potency. Through the interiorization of breath, they become gradually energized, pacified and purified, until each vibrates at the junction of its two distinctive poles. Once this junction is established, the attunement and harmonization of the centers that ensue, together with the bliss peculiar to each, bring about the fusion of all the purified—though still individual—energies. This phase corresponds to the Path of activity.

In this setting of well-balanced, appeased energies, the rising Kuṇḍalinī intensifies her work of unification. Under the pretext of an overwhelming emotion, fright or enjoyment, the thought-free energies converge at once toward the single center, stretching the individual limits to the point where subject and object fuse together. At this stage, the combination of sound, breaths, word, and intuitive knowledge results in knowledge of and mastery over the energies, and in a plenitude of union whose impetus merges together minor and main centers, devotee and deity, Śiva and Śakti. The purified organs gain access to the universal and may henceforth be used by way of a spring-board for the supreme passage into the oneness of pure Consciousness, when the cognitive energy converts into pure Self-awareness. Therein lies the consummation of the Path of energy.

Indeed through this union one is propelled into the oneness of the Divine Path; the universe unfolds again, but now transfigured and beyond interiority and exteriority.

Henceforth Kuṇḍalinī as impeller of energy is no more, nor the perception of a vibration which can no longer be distinguished from the immutable, *spanda* being melted in it. Individual, energy, and Śiva are but one; body and universe now appear as distinct on the background of supreme Consciousness wherein everything is integrated. The cosmic energy expands freely through the great centers of vibration, infusing into them the bliss of Consciousness. The individual organs function in such an impersonal manner that nothing more stands in the way of any form of oneness, and in such dynamism that no longer can one speak of static coincidence, of microcosm and macrocosm. The essential difference only lies between the dormant, separate, exteriorized energies and the unified, interiorized energies.

Thus the yogin, master of his energies through Kuṇḍalinī, shows that the human being holds within himself the source and the inexhaustible storehouse of his sovereignty, bliss and efficience.

And it is precisely in mystical efficience that the great unifying function of Kuṇḍalinī culminates—the keystone of transmission. Through the power and subtlety of his divinized energy, the *guru* gradually interiorizes and activates the scattered energies of the disciple, whose Kuṇḍalinī he awakens just as, one might say, a stringed instrument transmits its vibration all around.

Striking his own Kuṇḍalinī like a tuning fork, the master gives the keynote; he transmits the "right frequency."

As the register of his kundalinian energy covers all the harmonic progression of the fundamental vibration, he empowers the disciple to correctly tune in on the particular degree of the harmonic scale that agrees with him; he imparts to him both the initial impulse and the harmonized tonality.

Thus attuned to and by the master, the disciple's Kuṇḍalinī rises from wheel to wheel, moving up the scale toward the more and more subtle harmonics of the *spanda.* Just as a tuned musical instrument can make others vibrate in unison, through mere resonance, so the master now makes the awakened heart of the disciple resonate continuously, thus transforming his listening-in aptitude and the acuteness of his hearing.

The disciple experiences his capacity of resonance as increasing, his harmonic register amplifying, and he receives with an ever-expanding consciousness what is given him by the master until complete fusion is achieved wherein all the notes merge into one single note, master and disciple being now but one instrument, one music, one consciousness.

We shall conclude with stanzas from the *Cidgaganacandrikā,* "resplendent moonlight in the firmament of Consciousness" cited by Maheśvarānanda[1] and offered to the Mother—Kuṇḍalinī.

1. M.M., pp. 131–137 of my translation.

A tribute to the various *mudrā,* this hymn describes and extols five great mystical attitudes corresponding to five groups of *siddha.* Having recognized the Self and become endowed with Knowledge, they attain fusion in the Whole through an ascent of Kuṇḍalinī which starts from different *cakra* according to each one's specific *mudrā.* Only the last two groups, having reached perfect Knowledge, also enjoy power.

> "O Mother, the whole body with all its organs, inside as well as outside, Thou dost bring them all to the void of Consciousness. Such is to us the *karaṅkinī* attitude."

The *karaṅkinī* attitude (the repose of death), consisting of prolonged quietude and immobility, is that of the *jñānasiddha* "given over to knowledge," who concentrate on the inferior *cakra*; they resort to this attitude apt to interiorize the organs just as these come into contact with their respective sense-objects, for they wish their everyday activity to be pervaded by their appeased and illumined Consciousness.

> "O Mother, when Thou wantest to resorb all the levels of reality, from earth to primordial nature—in other words, the limited perception—Thou assumest the form of mantra and Thou standest with gaping mouth. Then Thou art the Wrathful, Krodhanī."

The *krodhanī* attitude, that of wrath, pertains to the *mantrasiddha* who, swallowing objects and notions, incorporate them in their own undifferentiated essence and become "masters of the formulas"; their Kuṇḍalinī moves up from the navel.

> "O Umā! . . . She is situated in the empty sky of the Consciousness free of all veil. She contains the whole differentiation in its form of vibration, she mingles with the whole, and this Bhairavī Thou art."

To define the *bhairavīmudrā,* Maheśvarānanda adds a stanza of his own:

The energies—attributes of the great Union (*mahāmelāpa*)—assume the form of the awakening of Kuṇḍalinī; residing in the realm of the void of the Consciousness free of all veil, they shine there eternally. Beyond being and non-being, this energy, appearing in the glorious effulgence of her unveiled form, is the one called *bhairavīmudrā,* that pervades the multiplicity of the differentiated objects born of her intense power and protects the oneness endowed with immutable flavor and undisturbed expansion. Ever "sealed," belonging to the goddesses who excel at union (*melāpa*), this *mudrā* is twofold: internally or externally "sealed"; and here is described the external seal, the Splendor attitude, which is no other than *bhairavīmudrā.*

The famous *bhairavīmudrā* is the mystical attitude of the *melāpasiddha,* who are given over to union—union of Śiva and the energy, union of the *siddha* and the *yoginī*; they resorb everything into a fully expanded and active Consciousness. In their case Kuṇḍalinī starts from the heart *cakra.*

"The collection of rays engaged in absorbing the dross of the subtle body licks and consumes differentiation in its flames; it is Thou, O Mother, who, licking with great force, experiencest the *lelihānīmudrā.*"

The so-called *lelihānīmudrā* attitude, "the one who licks," belongs to the *śāktasiddha*, masters of the energy. By its means they destroy the last remnants of the differentiated. Freed from all attachment, they are autonomous in their sexual practice and may unite with their own wives. They raise their Kuṇḍalinī from the throat *cakra*.

"O Goddess, Thou art engaged in destroying speech, which ranges from the Word down to ordinary speech. Free from all veil, Thou reachest the abode of Śiva and revealest Thyself as the one roaming in the firmament of Consciousness (*khecarī*) and bringing about its unfolding. O Mother! Thou art this *Kuṇḍalī* who soarest up like a flash of lightning and eagerly devourest the brilliance of fire, sun, and moon. When Thou breakest Thy path through the middle way, in *KHA,* up to the *śāmbhavasiddha bindu,* Thou art known as Khecarī."

The *śāmbhavasiddha,* devoted to Śiva, transcends the couple Śiva-Śakti; he does not accept any second, and in oneness he blends knowledge and power. In his case, Kuṇḍalinī rises from the mid-eyebrows center (*bhrū*) beyond the *suṣumnā,* as the all-pervading cosmic Consciousness, freed from thought (*unmanā*).

Compared to those previously described, his attitude, the *khecarīmudrā,* is transcendental: the fully unfolded energy wanders unimpeded in infinite Consciousness, in *kha.* As neither interiorized nor exteriorized consciousness is any longer distinct, such a *siddha,* outwardly, can no longer be distinguished from an ordinary human being.

In order to show how the *mudrā* which "seals" in Consciousness performs its task without gradation and enables the *siddha* to recover the Whole instantly, Maheśvarānanda compares it to the miraculous tree of love, which is identical to Śiva and has no need to grow:

"The celestial tree, with its strong branches of awareness, is already fully grown in the realm of the heart. Its blossom is the glowing rapture, its fruit the exhilarating joy of unalloyed bliss."[2]

And from this heart—the bedrock of the universe—rises the axis of Kuṇḍalinī.

Thus the creeping, subterranean, obscure energy shoots up, and like an immobile and vibrant pillar piercing its way through space, it roots the sky in the earth. Then, as Khecarī, it soars up

2. M.M. 52, p. 160.

and roams with total freedom in the infinite firmament of Consciousness.

Ahirbudhnya, the invisible serpent of the depths, jealously guarding the primal waters of Life, envelops the universe in its circles of mists and should be recognized and revered as this primordial, eternal cosmic axis, the one-footed UNBORN, Aja-Ekapāda.

INDEX OF SANSKRIT TERMS

Ojas: Virile potency stored up in the yogin's body, 3, 161.
OṂ: The *praṇava,* mystic syllable, 46–47, 90, 191; its twelve stages, 49.

Kanda: Lower bulb at the root of the *nāḍī,* 73, 106, 130.
Kaṇṭha: Throat center, 28.
Kampa: Trembling occuring in the heart, 73, 163.
Kalā: Subtle energy, 20, 98, 107, 130, 201.
Kāma: Worldly desire; god of desire and love, 140, 161.
Kālāgni: Destroying fire of time.
Kālī: Divine energy, 9.
Kumbhaka: Breath retention, 32, 122.
Kuṇḍalinī or *kuṇḍalī:* Energy of breath and of *vīrya,* 63, 69; *prāṇakuṇḍalinī,* 64; *cid kuṇḍalinī,* Kuṇḍalinī of Consciousness, 64. *Śaktikuṇḍalinī, Kuṇḍalinī* of energy, 21–22.
Kula: Its different meanings, 19; as undivided whole, 187; *Kulacārya* or sexual practice, *kulayāga* or *ādikula, kula* rite, 157, 177, 180; *Kulamārga:* esoteric way, 157.
Kaula: Ultimate Reality, 169, 188; *Kaulikīśakti:* divine energy, 171.
Krama: Progression: *Kramamudrā:* mystical attitude equalizing within and without, 30, 60, 170; *Kramamudrāsamatā:* achieved equality, 61, 170.
Kriyā: Activity, 129; *Kriyāśakti:* divine energy at work in this world, 58, 145, 154.
Kṣobha: Agitation, effervescence, stirring, 7, 22, 161, 186.
Kha or *khe:* Etheric void, hub of the wheel of energies, space at the center of the heart, 8, 153, 212; vibration of the heart, 7; *Khecarī:* energy freely roaming in the ether of Consciousness. *Khecarī mudrā:* corresponding mystical attitude, 131, 200, 211–212.

Gagana: Spatial infinity, 3, 153.
Gāndhārī: name of a *nāḍī,* 124, 130
Garbha: Womb, 126.
Ghūrṇi: Intense vibration inducing a state of dizziness and inebriation, 30, 58, 74.

Cakra: Wheel, center through which Kuṇḍalinī moves, 25, 31, 183.
Catuṣpada: Crossroad of the four ways of ordinary and subtle breaths, 28.
Candrārdha: Half-moon, one of the sound energies of *OṂ,* 49, 202.
Candramaṇḍala: Circle of the moon.
Camatkāra: Enraptured seizure, cry of suprise, wonder, 72.
Caryākrama: Esoteric practice, xvi, 157, 171.
Cit, citi: Pure Consciousness, 8, 114.
Citriṇī: One of the *nāḍī.*

Jagat: Universe, 102; *Jagadānanda:* universal bliss, 77, 167.
Janmasthāna: Place of birth, 146, 174; *Janmādhāra,* 27, 111, 154.
Japa: Recitation, resonance related to inner utterance, 197.
Jīva: Life, 39, *Jīvātman:* limited being, individual, 131.
Jñāna: Mystical knowledge, 129, 154.

Tantra or *āgama:* Sacred texts of the Śaiva schools.
Tālu: A point situated in the palate, 57, 68–69, 128.
Tejas: Effulgence of Consciousness, 72, 128.
Turya: Fourth state, beyond waking, sleeping, and dreaming = absorption with closed eyes, 64, 154.
Turyātīta: Beyond all state, 64, 154, 167.
Trika: System of the triad: Śiva, Energy and individual; knower, knowledge and known; the three corresponding paths of liberation: etc., 105.

Bhāvana: Mystical practice, 53.
Bhairava: Undifferentiated Śiva, pp. 7, 55, 68, 145; who swallows the universe, 61.
Bhairavī: Energy (*śakti*) of Bhairava, 8; *Bhairavī mudrā:* mystical attitude equalizing two poles, 8, 210.
Bhrama: Vortex of brahman, 43.
Bhrūmadhya: Mid-eyebrows center, 28, 69.
Bhrūvedha: Initiatory piercing relating to the *bindu*, 29.
Bhrūvedhakṣepa: Scattering of the energies contained in *bhrū*, 29.

Madhya: Middle, interval, central point; *Madhyanāḍī:* median conduit or *suṣumnānāḍī*, 125, 196; *Madhyacakra:* central wheel, 139, 172.
Mantra: Mystic formula, 197. See also *Aham, OṂ, Sauḥ, Kha. Mantra dīkṣā:* Initiation by means of the mantra, 93.
Manthana: Churning leading to the dissolution of all things in Consciousness, 7, 60.
Maṇīpūra: Name of a *cakra* meaning "abundance of jewels," 127.
Maṇḍala: Diagram, 203. Fire, sun, and moon circles, 131.
Mahānanda: Great bliss, 76.
Mahāvyāpti: Great pervasion, 56, 76, 174.
Mahārasa: Great savor of a mystical nature, 175.
Mātṛkā: Seed-letters, phonemes, phonetic energies, 32, 112, 131.
Mithuna: Sexual union, 143.
Mudrā: Seal of unity, indelible mark, 210–212.
Mūlakanda: Bulb situated at the base or at the root, 27.
Mūlādhāra: Root support, 26, 33, 69, 128. Inferior center equivalent to *janmādhāra* and *kulamūla*, 26, 33, 69.
Melaka: Great mystical gatherings, 165.
Melana, melāpa: Union of *yoginī* and *vīra*, 211.

Yāmala: Union, 20. *Yāmala cakra:* wheel of mystical union, that of Śiva and Śakti, 10, 19, 201.
Yoginī: Deity, 158. Yogin's divinized energies, 159, 166. Partner of a *siddha* or a *vīra*, 137. *Yoginībhū:* exceptional child born from a pure womb, 174, 179, 199. *Yoginī vaktra:* mouth of the *yoginī*, universal womb, 27, 173.

Rasa: Savor, 175.
Rahasya: Mystic, arcane, secret, 177, 203, 204.
Rudra: Another name for Śiva, 10. *Rudra yāmala:* union of the divine couple, 137, 162, 170, 173, 185.

Lalāṭa: Forehead, 28–30.
Lakṣaṇa: Symptom, 107.
Liṅga: Sign, the three *liṅga*, 126, 144, 199–200, 203.
Lambikā: Uvula, "that which is hanging," 28, 56, 126.

Vāyu: Air, vital breath.
Vikalpa: Dualizing thought, dilemma, differentiation, pp. 38, 163.
Vikāsa: Expansion (of energy), 199.
Vimarśa: Act of awareness, Self-consciousness, 7, 19, 21.
Viṣa: Poison, omnipenetration, 15, 52, 125, 140.
Viśrānti: Appeasement, 53, 79.
Visarga: Emission, 152, 187. Triple, 19. Cosmic, 21. Seminal, 171. Symbolic sign, two points one above the other, 22, 168.
Vīra: Hero who has conquered his senses and thoughts, 157.

ABBREVIATIONS AND WORKS

I.P.K. *Iśvarapratyabhijñākārikā* by Utpaladeva. Kashmir Series of Texts and Studies, no. 34, Śrīnagar, 1921.

I.P.v. *Iśvarapratyabhijñāvimarśinī* by Abhinavagupta. K.S.T.S. nos. 22 and 33, 1918 and 1921.

M.M. *Mahārthamañjarī de Maheśvarānanda, avec des extraits du Parimala.* Traduction et Introduction par Lilian Silburn, Paris, Ed. de Boccard, 1968.
Mahārthamañjarī. Ed. by Gaṇapati Śāstrī, Trivandrum Skt. Series no. 66, 1919.

M.V. *Mālinīvijayottaratantra.* K.S.T.S., no. 37, Bombay, 1922.

N.T. *Netratantra,* with the commentary by Kṣemarāja, 2 vols. K.S.T.S., nos. 46 and 61, Bombay, 1926 and 1939.

P.H. *Pratyabhijñāhṛdaya.* Ed. by J.C. Chatterjee, K.S.T.S., no. 3, Śrīnagar, 1911.
Pratyabhijñāhṛdaya. Saṃskṛta text with English translation and notes by Jaideva Singh, Delhi: M. Banarsidass, 1963.

P.S. *Paramārthasāra d'Abhinavagupta.* Texte sanskrit édité et traduit par Lilian Silburn. Paris, 1957 and 1979.

P.T.v. *Parātriṃśikāvivaraṇa* by Abhinavagupta. K.S.T.S., no. 18, Śrīnagar, 1918.
Parātrīśikālaghuvṛtti de Abhinavagupta. Texte traduit et annoté par A. Padoux, Paris, 1975.
Skt. edition: K.S.T.S., no. 68. Śrīnagar, 1947.

S.D. *Śivadṛṣti* by Somānanda, with the commentary by Utpaladeva. K.S.T.S., no. 54, Śrīnagar, 1934.

S.K. *Spandakārikā* by Vasugupta, with the commentary by Rāmakaṇṭha. K.S.T.S., no. 6, Śrīnagar, 1913.

Sn. *Spandanirṇaya* by Kṣemarāja. Text and English translation, K.S.T.S., no. 42, Śrīnagar, 1925.

Sc. *Stavacintāmaṇi de Bhaṭṭa Nārāyaṇa, La Bhakti.* Texte traduit et commenté par Lilian Silburn. Paris, 1964 and 1979.

S.S.v. *Śivasūtrasvimarśinī* by Kṣemarāja. K.S.T.S., no. 1, Śrīnagar, 1911. And ed. by P.N. Pushp, 1973.

____ *Śivasūtra et Vimarśinī de Kṣemarāja.* Introduction et traduction par Lilian Silburn. Paris, 1980.

____ *Śiva Sūtras, The Yoga of Supreme Identity.* Text and *vimarśini*. Translated by Jaideva Singh. Delhi, 1979.

S.st. *Śivastotrāvali* by Utpaladeva, with the commentary by Kṣemarāja. Ed. by Rājanaka Lakṣmaṇa, Chowkhamba Sanskrit Series, Benares, 1964.

Sv. *Svacchanda Tantra,* with the commentary by Kṣemarāja, 7 vols. K.S.T.S. Bombay, 1921–1935.

T.A. *Tantrāloka* by Abhinavagupta with the commentary by Jayaratha, 12 vols. K.S.T.S. Śrīnagar-Bombay, 1918–1938.

V.B. *Vijñānabhairava.* Texte traduit et commenté par Lilian Silburn. Paris, 1961, 1976 and 1983.

____ *Vijñānabhairava or Divine Consciousness. A Treasury of 112 types of Yoga.* Text and English Translation by Jaideva Singh. Delhi: M. Banarsidass, 1979.

____ *Recherches sur la Symbolique et l'énergie de la parole dans certains textes tantriques.* André Padoux. Paris, Ed. E. de Boccard, 1963.

____ *L'énergie de la Parole.* André Padoux. Le Soleil Noir, 1980.

——— *Luce delle Sacre Scritture (Tantrāloka) di Abhinavagupta.* Translated by Raniero Gnoli, Torino, 1972.

——— *Haṭhayogapradīpikā.* Traduction, introduction et notes. Tara Michaël. Fayard, 1974.

——— *Corps subtil et corps causal. Les six cakra et le kuṇḍalinī yoga.* Tara Michaël. Courrier du Livre, 1979.

——— *Upanishads du Yoga.* Traduites du sanskrit et annotées par Jean Varenne. Gallimard, 1971.